A STRENGTH NOT MY OWN

LeRoy Lawson

STANDARD PUBLISHING
Cincinnati, Ohio

Unless otherwise noted, all Scripture quotations are from the *Holy Bible: New International Version*, ©1973, 1978, 1984 by the International Bible Society. Used by permission of Zondervan Bible Publishers.

Library of Congress Cataloging in Publication data:

Lawson, E. LeRoy, 1938 –
    A strength not my own / LeRoy Lawson.
        p.   cm.
    ISBN 0-87403-746-8
    1. Christian life – 1960-   2. Consolation.   3. Lawson, E. LeRoy,
1938-   .   I. Title.
BV4501.2.L3656   1992
248.4 – dc20   91-35751
                                                    CIP

Copyright © 1992. The STANDARD PUBLISHING Company, Cincinnati, Ohio.
A division of STANDEX INTERNATIONAL Corporation. Printed in U.S.A.

CONTENTS

INTRODUCTION

This book is the most personal I have written, which is saying a lot, since I have been pretty transparent in earlier ones. In those books, though, I limited myself to a personal anecdote or allusion here and there. This study is different. The whole theme is more personal, more confessional, than I have tried to write before.

The cause of this more autobiographical approach is the Scripture that inspires the book. When Phyllis Sanders, who by now has dispensed most of my assignments for Standard Publishing Company, described what she wanted me to write this time, she used words like "fitness," "strength," and even "muscular." She told me she wanted a book about the power available to us Christians, but then she said something like, "But make it clear we're not talking about something we do to make ourselves strong, but instead that this power is ours through the grace of God."

The words "with a strength not my own" and the text 2 Corinthians 12:7-10 instantly leapt into mind. I couldn't hide my enthusiasm for the project. I've been meditating on this theme all my life.

Sometimes Christians "claim" a certain Scripture for a day, or they memorize a text for a week or a month. I've often done the same. But many years ago, I adopted these verses, especially the last words ("For when I am weak, then I am strong," 2 Corinthians 12:10) as *my* special Scripture for life. Of all the Bible verses I've treasured, these are the words that have most often been my "bridge over troubled waters." When I feel my weakest, they remind me I can draw on a strength not my own.

Not, you understand, that I could ever equal the apostle Paul's claim in the preceding verses. I've never been "caught up to the third heaven" (verse 2). I've had no private viewing of paradise. My feet have never left the earth "whether in the body or apart from the body" (verse 2). There is very little of the mystic in me; of ecstatic experiences I have nothing to boast. Mine tends to be a pretty pragmatic, workaday, plodding kind of faith.

Thus I can't profess kinship with the writer of the first six verses of 2 Corinthians 12, but when Paul writes of a "thorn in my flesh, a messenger of Satan" (verse 7) that could not be exorcised through prayer, and when he boasts of his weaknesses, he speaks to (and of) my condition.

In the eleventh chapter, Paul defends himself from critics who attack his apostolic credentials. Like them, he can brag about his Hebrew ancestry, his service record, and his perseverance through dangers and persecutions. In spite of every obstacle, and in spite of his personal weaknesses, he has been a dynamic instrument of God. Paul can't accept any credit, however, because, as far as he is concerned, he hasn't earned any. Whatever he has done, it was really God doing it through him.

This might sound like false humility, but it isn't. I didn't understand the passage for a long time. Like many other superficial Bible students, I squirmed a little when reading through several portions of 2 Corinthians. Sometimes what Paul writes seems precipitously close to arrogance. It isn't, though. He's not boasting; he's marveling.

Perhaps my current understanding is too heavily colored by astonishment at what God has done for me and through me, things I not only never imagined possible but could never even have imagined at all. (I could have written Ephesians 3:20, "Now to him who is able to do immeasurably more than all we ask or imagine. . . ." Events in my life have certainly outdistanced my imagination.) A "possibility thinker" I have never been. I have to be shown. And I have been!

Let me give you just one example of the incredible in my life. He's given me health. This assertion probably won't impress you, especially if you are in reasonably good health, but I have to tell you how good it feels to feel good. I can play and work strenuously, and I like it.

As an underweight, asthmatic little boy, unable to run around a baseball diamond or swim a pool length without fighting for oxygen, I was banned from a kid's normal outdoor games because I couldn't keep up. Instead of tumbling over a football field or racing around a track, I spent solitary hours exploring the fields and creeks and reading everything I could get my hands on. Whenever there was choosing up sides to play ball, the captains reluctantly chose me last—always. I was a deficit to any team. It wasn't an unhappy childhood, but I did often wonder how I would ever be able to lead a normal adult life.

Down the road from me lived an adult named John, also asthmatic. He couldn't work, even though he was nearly thirty; he still lived with his parents, who had to support him because he didn't have breath to do anything productive. In him I saw my future.

By the time I entered high school, I was less afraid, although still not able to do anything on the playing field. Too social to be a recluse, I participated in every activity my limitations would allow. By my teen years, I had learned there was much I could do. Football and other team sports may have been forbidden, but I had already learned that there's life after (and without) sports. My big regret in those years was feeling I was a disappointment to my father, since he had played everything he could as a youngster and still enjoyed a good game of baseball even though he was so old. (He was in his forties!)

In other words, I was what my children insist I was (whenever they look at my old high-school yearbooks), the original "nerd": bespectacled, bookish, and, they not so secretly suspect, boring.

Boring, perhaps, but not bored. "The theater" had captured me. In one way or another, you could have found me in those days either on stage or behind the scenes of most of our school's productions. Thanks to a superb teacher who recruited me to work on the school newspaper, I also quickly fell in love with journalism (a love affair that only diminished when greater experience taught me to doubt much of what appears in the papers). Thanks to my parents' dogged insistence, I was also still taking piano lessons and, for two years, played for a couple of the high school choirs, although I suspect my performance never afforded the directors much peace of mind as they conducted. I also dabbled a bit in science and was surprised to receive the chemistry award my senior year.

Drama, journalism, music, science—definitely the occupations of a first-class nerd.

To top it all off, I was super active, along with some of my best friends, in our church's youth program. In fact, as I now reflect on those days, I realize how much I am indebted to the nurturing of the church, beginning clear back in the preschool department. Throughout my growing years, those saints gave me the courage to keep trying when my self-confidence wavered, which it frequently did. At our church, they didn't laugh at nerds. Instead they encouraged the development of any talent we had, like the leadership ability they insisted they saw in me.

Later, when my parents' marriage was breaking up, I found solace in surrogate parents in the congregation who kept me from straying. In our youth group, also, we were taught that it was permissible to confess fears and doubts and to explore the larger questions of the meaning of life.

I realize I may be romanticizing the past a bit. I've reached that age.

But in this fact I'm not merely expressing my dotage: like the apostle Paul, I can enthusiastically boast, at long last, about my weaknesses. What for years I accepted as irritating liabilities in my constitution (an underwhelming physical stature, innumerable allergies, athletic non-prowess, even a weak voice) have turned out to be, when offered to God, not liabilities at all. From my experience, I have gained one of the firmest of my religious convictions, which is that when we hand God our handicaps and weaknesses, He transforms and returns them as strengths and assets.

That conviction is what this book is about.

"For when I am weak, then I am strong."

Let me leave the personal now; I've lingered too long over these memories. As I said, I've reached that age. You'll have noted that I haven't mentioned any dramatic healing or traumatic religious conversion. I have nothing of that kind to tell. Instead, mine is just the story of one who has always been weak, but who has found a strength not his own.

I want to tell you about it.

1

WITH A STRENGTH NOT MY OWN

2 Corinthians 12:1-10

In my day, there were giants in the land. We had heroes back when I was a kid, military and political leaders we believed in. The good guys were General Dwight Eisenhower, President Franklin Roosevelt, and Prime Minister Winston Churchill, who strode larger than life across the newsreels at the theater. The bad guys were equally awesome: Adolf Hitler, Joseph Stalin (good guy or bad guy, depending on the phase of the war), Emperor Hirohito, and Mussolini. Yes, we believed in heroes then, and we expected them to be mighty in battle and majestic in peace.

Today's young people aren't as naive about their leaders. Yellow journalism has systematically destroyed all illusions of grandeur. They have been taught to find Achilles' heel in every idol; there is none righteous, no not one. Doing away with heroes unfortunately wipes out faith in heroism. Muddling through is what we expect— and get. Everybody assumes that all persons are created equal—equally selfish, equally incompetent, equally weak. We have resigned ourselves to mediocrity—in government, in education, in business, . . . in persons.

On the one hand, we have to admit that everybody *is* weak. But even if that statement is true (and it is), we must hasten to add that not all weaknesses are equal. There is, thank God, a frailty that makes for strength.

It is of that form of weakness the apostle Paul writes. His words are the inspiration of this book. "For when I am weak, then I am strong" (2 Corinthians 12:10).

Where Did Paul Get His Confidence?

In his second letter to the Corinthians, Paul is unusually open about his human limitations. While basing his faith on the *objective* truth that Jesus is the Son of God and Savior of Man, he confesses the *subjective* nature of his faith as well. He writes from experience. He knows what he is talking about because he has "been there."

> I know a man in Christ who fourteen years ago was caught up to the third heaven. Whether it was in the body or out of the body I do not know—God knows. And I know that this man—whether in the body or apart from the body I do not know, but God knows—was caught up to Paradise. He heard inexpressible things, things that man is not permitted to tell (2 Corinthians 12:2-4).

This supernatural revelation cannot be conveyed in words; they can't carry such glory. If ever a man would have reason to boast, this man has.

How carefully Paul speaks of it. The message is in the verb's passive voice. The fantastic event wasn't something he *did or could do*; it was something *done to him and for him*. He deserves no credit at all.

Think what some latter-day "evangelist" might have made of this experience. A fortune could be milked from visions like this one, especially since, as Paul insists in the sixth verse, it's the truth. Unlike your average religious entrepreneur, he wouldn't be lying, wouldn't even be exaggerating. The public would pay dearly for this first-hand report from Heaven!

But Paul won't exploit his advantage. In fact, he doesn't even give us the full scoop, "so no one will think more of me than is warranted by what I do or say" (verse 6).

The truth is he saw paradise. But the truth is also he couldn't take any credit for the phenomenon. It wasn't by his power. It wasn't even by his initiative. He could never have pulled off something so remarkable on his own.

Then, as if Heaven were guaranteeing Paul could never preen over the experience, he says God handicapped him, "to keep me from becoming conceited" (verse 7).

Do you suppose that's the reason, in spite of all my prayers, God let me keep on wheezing? I asked so many times for release, but it did not come, at least not then, when I was pleading. Nor for a long time to come.

And do you suppose there's a reason now, so many years after I accepted my precarious health as my lot in life, that I almost never have to gasp for breath anymore? Instead, I enjoy a robust health exceeding my fondest hopes as a child. Not that everything is perfect. I seem to have outgrown my childhood infirmities just in time to make way for the natural disabilities of age. The asthma is virtually gone, thus leaving me free to concentrate on the less threatening, but nonetheless exasperating, symptoms of arthritis and other AARP-related irritants.

That's my problem, not Paul's. We don't really know what Paul's thorn in the flesh was. There are many guesses, of course: ophthalmia (eye disease), malaria, or some other physical ailment. Others have guessed it to be an emotional or psychosomatic problem of some kind. Still others spiritualize it. We simply don't know.

We do know that thorns aren't unusual. Nearly all mature Christians I have interviewed on this subject have admitted to some kind of disability that they have asked God to remove, but He hasn't. They feel their affliction weakens them; most of them have found it has also, in some way, strengthened them.

Forgive me for becoming personal again, but I want to confess what this thorn now symbolizes for me.

In the beginning, it was a physical one, sapping my body of normal strength.

Now it's not physical.

When I was a young man, I took my vows of ordination. It was a somber moment when I knelt for the elders to lay their hands on me. With all my heart, I was giving myself to God's work. He was going to have all I have, all I am. For His sake I was going to work to become the best. With all that was in me, I was ready to become as nearly a perfect minister as God wanted me to be.

I let Him down. My very best turned out not to be so very much.

When Joy and I stood before her minister father as he led us through our marriage vows, I meant every word I promised. I was really in love and felt fortunate this beautiful woman had consented to be my wife. I didn't consider myself a great catch; as a product of a broken home, I felt unqualified to lead my own family. I was determined, though, to give as much to be a perfect husband as I could possibly give.

It turned out not to be much.

And so it has been from that day until now. I wanted to be the perfect father, too, but ended up far from the mark on that one.

As a matter of fact, everything that, as a young man, I wanted to be able to boast about when I reached the age I am now, I have marred in one way or another. There's nothing left to brag about.

By now I'm not certain exactly what my thorn is. I just know that whichever of the many possibilities it is, it has (or all of them together have) been sufficient "to keep me from becoming conceited." Like Paul, I have to admit that whatever strength I have is not in myself. Like him, if I have anything to boast of, it has to do with weakness.

What Is the Source of His Humility?

Do you think Paul, after his ecstasy in paradise, could ever have contained his crowing if he had also enjoyed unbroken success in prayer? Suppose God had removed his thorn? Wouldn't this former Pharisee now have had all the proof he could ever need of his spiritual superiority? Couldn't he silence his enemies then? They hadn't had even a peep into the third heaven, had they? From what we know of Paul from his other letters and the Acts account, we have no trouble appreciating a well placed thorn's value in taming a personality like his.

Several years ago *Time* published some revealing statistics. It reported that every year 36 to 77 of every 100,000 physicians in our country commit suicide, three times the rate of the general population. According to the article, physicians join dentists, lawyers, and police officers as the most "self-destructive" professionals. Los Angeles psychiatrist Robert Litman offers this explanation: "They believe themselves to be omnipotent, semi-deities in a white smock."[1] (He has to be referring to the minority of these professionals; most are surely not guilty of his charge.) It's not easy playing God. After trying it for a while and failing, the physicians have to admit they are failing. Omnipotence is beyond them. So they turn, the article says, to drugs, alcohol, psychotherapy, and eventually suicide.

I once observed the decline and fall of a brilliant, successful physician. He abandoned his practice in mid-career to pursue a new profession on a college campus. Before moving to his new location he asked my advice. I hesitantly offered it. "You're used to being God," I told him, none too tactfully. "You won't get the same kind of respect from students you have received from your patients. In fact, you won't get any respect at all just because of your position. Can you take it?"

Yes, he insisted. But he couldn't. He had lived too long without thorns.

He could have used a little dose of the wisdom of Abraham Lincoln, who told his friend Noah Brooks, "I am very sure that if I do not go away from here [the White House] a wiser man, I shall go away a better man, for having learned here what a very poor sort of man I am."[2]

This is what Paul has learned. He's the sort of man with whom God has been able to do some wonderful things — but not without thorns.

Paul's enforced humility profited him much. Such modesty, as someone has keenly observed, gives one the ability to endure suffering without complaining, "I don't deserve this." It is also the ability to enjoy blessings and not gloat, "I do deserve these."

What Is This Thing Called Grace?

What we've really been exploring, without saying so yet, is the experience of grace. The Lord said it specifically to Paul: "My grace is sufficient for you, for my power is made perfect in weakness" (verse 9).

Here is one of God's great promises, one that so-called self-made, self-sufficient persons don't know anything about and don't even know they are missing. It's the secret of the bethorned.

Roland Bainton's father is a good example. Professor Bainton, one of America's greatest church historians, once paid this tribute to his father, a humble, contented pastor whose congregations never numbered more than 200:

Early he realized that he would never play a conspicuous role in the life of the Church. Had he been invited to a renowned pulpit he could not have accepted by reason of the infirmities of the flesh. He suffered from glandular tuberculosis in college, and though this was surmounted he continued to be sickly. . . . One thus hampered could not have carried a major assignment. [He] knew it and was not cankered by jealousy, tormented by ambition or racked by frustration. Within the framework of frailty he aimed at excellence, reminding himself that . . . "'the wayside pool reflects the fleeting clouds as exactly as does the mighty ocean."[3]

The gentle pastor had found the secret of living. "Contented," free from jealousy, ambition, and frustration. Yet he pursued personal excellence and lived to reflect the glory of God. He had found grace.

Grace in this verse is divine energy enabling us to surmount weakness and thus live victoriously, fruitfully, and contentedly. It is both a resting and a rising: resting in the sovereignty and kindness of God, so that "Christ's power may rest on me" (verse 9), and rising to the challenge weakness offers, refusing to grant it sovereignty. It is the experience of a strength not our own, granted not in spite of, but because of, our weakness.

Awareness of how God's universe operates helps us appreciate grace. Growing up along the Pacific Northwest coast gave me an opportunity to observe the myriad little beach animals. Our family often searched the beach for sand dollars, cockles and mussels, clams and barnacles, starfish, and other fascinating forms of marine life. We quickly learned that the turbulent ocean water, which with its pounding breakers and ebbing and flowing tides made life so difficult for the delicate creatures, at the same time was keeping them alive. The pounding water that threatened their comfort brought them food and oxygen and carried their larva seaward.

So in the nature of things, these weak little creatures live a life of blessing mixed with difficulties, cradled in an environment in which they alternately rest and hustle. They might, if they could talk, speak of the thorn in their "flesh." On the other hand, they could give thanks for the grace that provides the food and oxygen.

Christians have learned there's more to their surrounding environment than meets the eye. They give thanks for their food and shelter and oxygen. They can even join Paul in giving thanks for their weaknesses. Among their other reasons for rejoicing is their knowing they have Someone to thank for His graciousness. You CAN frequently hear one of us exclaiming, "I don't know what I'd have done without prayer . . . without God . . . without my faith in God . . . without having God with me."

Oscar Wilde, a notorious literary figure in Victorian England, was apparently justly jailed on a morals charge. When released, he no longer wrote sparkling comedies nor skewered people with his famous wit. He had lost his heart for the superficial. It was in this sober post-prison period that he spoke his deepest truth: "Where there is sorrow, there is holy ground."

Christ meets us in our sorrow. His grace, always at hand but not always perceived, comforts us in our sadness, our discomfort, our weakness. *Comforts*. That's the word. It comes from the Latin and means "strengthened with." When He comforts us, we are no longer alone, but teamed up, the two of us. His strength and our weakness are harnessed together.

Where Do You Get This Surge of Power?

Paul's key concluding phrase is a familiar one: "for Christ's sake" (verse 10). These three words reveal the secret of his victory. He hasn't let his thorn monopolize his attention. His interest has been captured by Another.

His life is focused on a purpose that keeps him from exploiting his Paradise excursion even as it delivers him from despair over his disability. He has something — Someone — to live for far more important than either bragging about Heaven or bewailing his handicap. He does everything "for Christ's sake." He practiced what he preached to others: "So whether you eat or drink or whatever you do, do it all for the glory of God" (1 Corinthians 10:31). You bear your burden for Him, tolerate your thorns for Him; and it's all worthwhile because of Him.

Thornton Wilder, in his play *The Angel That Troubled the Waters*, captures Paul's meaning. The setting is beside a pool of water that, people believed, was periodically disturbed by an angel. (See John 5:1-15.) Whoever gets into the water first is healed. Among the crowd of people waiting the ruffling of the surface is a physician incurably ill. Though a healer himself, he has come seeking help from a strength greater than his own. As he pushes forward, an angel stops him. Healing is not for the physician, he tells him. Then, with an insight undoubtedly inspired by the apostle Paul, the angel adds,

> Without your wound where would your power be? It is your very remorse that makes your low voice tremble into the hearts of men. The very angels themselves cannot persuade the wretched and blundering children on earth as can one human being broken on the wheels of living. In Love's service only the wounded soldiers can serve. Draw back. . . .[4]

Another Physician once heard similar words, although no sympathetic angel spoke. Still another physician heard about the event and recorded it in his account of the Great Physician. "He saved others; let him save himself if he is the Christ of God, the Chosen One" (Luke 23:35). He couldn't, because "in Love's service only the wounded soldiers can serve." His service required more than a thorn in the flesh; it called for a whole crown of thorns and a spear.

Through His weakness, we all become strong.

> For we do not have a high priest who is unable to sympathize with our weaknesses, but we have one who has been tempted in every way, just as we are—yet was without sin. Let us then approach the throne of grace with confidence, so that we may receive mercy and find grace to help us in our time of need (Hebrews 4:15, 16).

This grace is available from the One who knows what we are going through—He went through it first. We draw strength from His experience. He stiffens our resolve. He props us up in our leaning places. When we think we have nothing to offer, He makes something useful of us.

Francis of Assissi, the humble monk who founded the Franciscan Order, understood this truth as well as anyone in Christian history. His insight once surprised his most devoted follower, Masseo, who had asked him, "You are not handsome, not learned; why then does all the world run after you?"

Francis explained that it was his lack of striking looks and learning that attracted people.

That is precisely why! It shows you that it is all the work of God. To prove the more strikingly that it is He who is at work, He has chosen me, the ugliest, the most wretched among his children, and the greatest sinner. Without God I am nothing.[5]

But with God he established a great service order, and with God became one of the most famous men in the history of western civilization. Had he been handsome or learned or powerful or wealthy, God could not have demonstrated his power through him

Because he was weak, God could make him strong

Because we are weak, God can—and if we let Him, He will—endow us with a strength not our own.

Notes

[1]*Time*, February 16, 1981, p. 57.

[2]Carl Sandburg, *Abraham Lincoln: The War Years*, Volume 3 (New York: Harcourt, Brace and Company, 1939), p. 381.

[3]Quoted in Robert J. McCracken, *Putting Faith to Work* (Carmel, New York: Guideposts Associates, 1960), pp. 95, 96.

[4]Quoted in John M. Krumm, *The Art of Being a Sinner* (New York: Seabury Press, 1967), pp. 85, 86.

[5]Rene Fulop-Miller, *The Saints That Moved the World* (Thomas Y. Crowell Company, 1945), p. 241.

2

WHEN I AM LITTLE, THEN I AM BIG

Psalm 139:1-3, 14-18; Matthew 18:2-4

My memories of my father come more from the time since I left home, than from my childhood. Because he worked so hard when I was still home, we didn't have enough time together. It was only later, in his final years, that our relationship really flourished. We became the best of friends. Of course, he never stopped acting like my father. He never intended to.

He made that clear to me when I had become a father myself. My lesson took place when Joy and I had been married four years and had been parents a year. Our wonderful Tigard church gave us several weeks' vacation, more time off than we had ever had. Like many young couples, we now had more time than money, so we traveled to Wyoming to visit my father and stepmother. We stayed ten days, which was too long. ("Fish and visitors stink in three days," Benjamin Franklin warns.) Toward the end of the sojourn, tensions had begun to rise.

The specific problem was our daughter Kim. My father was the kind of parent who, every night of the year, would get up in the middle of the night to check on us children (at least, that's what he said at the time; now that I have reached well into middle age, I suspect his nocturnal treks had another purpose). If he found we had kicked off our covers, he would lovingly replace them and return to his bed.

During our Wyoming visit, he performed this service for Kim. Every night as he checked on her, he found her uncovered. He replaced the covers, returned to his bed, and reported the next morning on what he found. He accompanied his report with a little lecture on the principles of good parenting, including the specific tenet concerning how, had we been good parents, we would have been checking on our daughter as well. Now Joy and I were the kind of parents who, when we went to sleep, intended to stay there for the rest of the night. We have always respected the right of our children to toss off their covers if that was how they preferred to sleep.

Along about the ninth morning, Dad's daily lecture had grown a little tiresome and, I'm sorry to confess, I talked back. It was only the second time in my life I can remember sassing him. Almost immediately I repented my words and, after a respectful interval, apologized. Then I explained, "But Dad, after being a preacher and a teacher and a husband and a father, it's tough going back to being a little boy again."

"Well," Dad said matter of factly, "you'll just have to get used to it."

And I did.

It's not easy for anybody to become a child again, which is what makes being "born again" so difficult. To return to the beginning, to take parental orders again, to admit to being less than fully formed, to abide by the rules of the Father's house—who said it would be easy? But you just have to get used to it.

And you can.

You must, if you would enter the kingdom of Heaven. The doors of the kingdom of God slam shut against anyone too proud to learn, too haughty to stoop, too strong to accept help, or too old to be a child again.

He called a little child and had him stand among them. And he said: "I tell you the truth, unless you change and become like little children, you will never enter the kingdom of heaven. Therefore, whoever humbles himself like this child is the greatest in the kingdom of heaven" (Matthew 18:2-4).

My dad was right. Without my willingness to become his child again, I could never be fully at ease in his home. And Jesus was right: without humbling ourselves like a child before our Heavenly Father, we can never dwell contentedly in His home, either.

When we do, we receive a strength not our own. "Consider the lilies of the field" (Matthew 6:28, KJV), Jesus teaches, because they are radiant in a strength not their own.

For that matter, consider the child. I've been doing this a lot lately, no longer with the harried, busy, devoted but distracted eyes of a parent, but from the loftier vantage of the grandfather who, though still busy, approaches a child more appreciatively, attentively, even eagerly now, as much to learn as to teach, for the child holds the key to mysteries marvelous.

What is it that children know, that this grandfather once knew but has long forgotten, knowledge so natural to children that they become in Jesus' teaching the model that adults must follow to be pleasing to God?

This used to be a hard question, when I was younger and trying so earnestly to rid myself of any vestige of childlikeness. Even when I became a parent, I didn't quite understand. It only takes a few sets of diapers to dispel any romantic notions one might have had of the perfectness of the newborn. Exhausted parents detect precious little worthy of imitation in their 3:00 AM torturer screaming from causes undiagnosed and calmed by nothing available.

But then comes grandparenthood. From this advanced perspective, Jesus makes sense. As I write these words, Joy and I have recently welcomed our second natural grandson into the world. (Perhaps I should explain that word "natural." You shouldn't infer that our others are unnatural. They aren't. They're just "borrowed," or unofficially "adopted," because years back we invited one of their parents to become a part of our family—and we've just never let go. So now we claim seven grandchildren in all—Stephanie, Tyler, Jake, Kristen, and Kim in addition to the "real" ones— but we are biologically responsible for only two of them.) First there was Kyle who, we were immediately persuaded, had surpassed all previous babies in brilliance, physical dexterity, and charisma. None could compare.

Then along came Nick, and in him we discovered, to our surprise, a whole new set of qualities to be described only in superlatives. How could one family possess so many powerful genes?

Of course, even if they were merely ordinary children, we'd still be speaking of the miracle of human birth. When we were parenting, we took the whole process pretty much for granted. Now, through grandparental eyes, it leaves us in awe.

Yet something else must be confessed about these grandsons of ours. If you were describing them, you might wax a little less enthusiastic. You might point out, especially if you weren't given to tact and diplomacy, that these peerless children of our children are weak, dependent, immature, incoherent, messy little disturbers of the peace, distinguishable in no extraordinary way from millions of other offspring you have seen.

Could Jesus have had such little ones in mind when He said we must become like children? Not really, I suppose. He was probably thinking of older ones, say around eight or ten. But even they are weak, aren't they? Would He have us exchange the advantages of maturity for all the disadvantages and liabilities of childhood?

What did the Lord mean, "unless you become like . . ."? I think I know. To answer, though, I will have to tell you a little more about my new grandson. I've been thinking a lot about him lately. He and his big brother Kyle are helping me to appreciate something of the strength in weakness that leads to, and comes from belonging to, the kingdom of God.

Here's what I see when I look at him.

I See His Uniqueness

We had the same fun with Nick as when his brother Kyle was born. We, his parents and grandparents, hovered over him, and indulged ourselves in the dividing of parts. Little was left of Nick by the time we had finished identifying our contributions. His mother claimed his disposition; his father, his coloring and the shape of his head and face; his grandmother definitely saw some of her Whitney family traits and contended he favored his uncle Lane. The nose, everyone agreed, was his grandfather's legacy, poor child.

We had our little fun at his expense; but of course, we, didn't take our game too seriously because Nick is, as Kyle before him, as all children before him, unique. There is, has been, and will never be another identical to him, anywhere, ever. His individuality is intact. He has not yet been molded into this world's form, conformed to this world's ways. He is who he is by the grace of the One who made him.

I See Fragility

Nick can't walk—can't even crawl yet. He can't talk, either, although he seems to make his elemental needs known. He can't dress or feed or clean himself. He even has to have help to burp. He seems the very epitome of weakness.

And yet—I can't get away with this. I remember when our firstborn, Nick's mother, arrived so many years ago. She was so tiny, so perfectly formed, so beautiful with her abundant hair and big, curious eyes. I was afraid to touch her. She might break.

When Kim's younger sister Candy was born, I paid more attention to the nurses in the hospital nursery. They grabbed the babies, tossed them upside down and yanked them around with incredible force. Yet none of them broke. They must have been a lot stronger than I thought. But when it was my turn to carry Candy, I held her as gingerly as I had Kim. By the time Candy's little brother Lane arrived, though, I could have worked in the nursery! I had begun to learn the lesson of this book, that surprising strength can be hidden within the apparently weak. So when I tell you I see fragility, I tell the truth, but not the whole truth.

I See Teachability

Even — or especially — in a newborn. As a matter of fact, you can't stop them from learning, at least under normal circumstances. Within days, infants learn to control the adults who attend them. They are, we grudgingly admire, "quick studies." They pay attention to everything around them and quickly adapt for survival — and conquest. Adults, on the other hand, can shut down their curiosity, and all too often do. It isn't unusual to discover among middle-aged and older people that their mental life has retired. They think no new thoughts, go no new places, try no new adventures. They merely serve their time until the end comes. Such are not of the kingdom of Heaven, not because God excludes them, but because they won't bestir themselves to check it out. They've seen enough in life, learned enough to satisfy themselves. They're through growing.

When I look at Nick's tiny frame, though, I don't so much see the baby that is as the man that will be.

I See Potentiality

His grandfather long ago reached manhood; most of what he would become was observable in the young adult. The remaining years have been more or less a working out of the predictable. But Nick—who knows what abilities God has given him, what opportunities lie in store, or what choices will be his to make? He is not yet what he will one day be. Yet in his genetic structure, the home environment into which he has been introduced, and the unforeseen circumstances that will swirl around him are to be found the ingredients of the making of Nicholas Denton. Nick's dominant verbs are in the future tense: he will become _____. My verbs, on the other hand, have shifted into the present; and it will not be long before the past tense will dominate my thinking and my writing and the sentences with which others will describe me: "Lawson? Oh, he was _____ back then."

Yet for candidates for the kingdom of Heaven, the future is ever ahead, beckoning onward and upward. Things are not now what they will be—and we are not yet what we will become. Like little children, we who would enter the kingdom remain mostly potential. "Now we see in a mirror dimly, but then face to face," is how the apostle Paul would express it (1 Corinthians 13:12, NASB). According to Jesus, death itself cannot change the verb into the past tense: He lived and he died and that's it? No. Jesus said, "Whoever lives and believes in me will never die" (John 11:26). Even at death, we, therefore, speak in the future (or permanent present) tense.

Further, to speak of *potential* is to speak of *power*. Already Nick is controlling the house, vying with his older brother for dominion. (His parents aren't even in the contest.) It is not without reason that the root of *potential* is *potens*, "power." Built into little babies from the moment sperm and egg unite is *potens*, power, and in all their early years that power shapes the becoming personality and the body that houses it. That power is, in a real sense, a strength not their own. It was given by their parents and their parents' parents, and their parents' parents' parents.

In one of the English language's most famous poems, William Wordsworth considers a child's potential and concludes, "The Child is Father of the Man. . . ." He regrets, however, that through the maturity process the natural piety and power of the child is lost. At first a child is at home in his newfound world:

> There was a time when meadow, grove, and stream,
> The earth, and every common sight,
> To me did seem
> Apparelled in celestial light,
> The glory and the freshness of a dream.

In time, however, he loses his ability to see and know the light:

> It is not now as it hath been of yore; —
> Turn wheresoe'er I may,
> By night or day,
> *The things which I have seen I now can see no more.*

> The Rainbow comes and goes,
> And lovely is the Rose;
> The Moon doth with delight
> Look round her when the heavens are bare;
> Waters on a starry night
> Are beautiful and fair;
> The Sunshine is a glorious birth;
> But yet I know, where'er I go,
> *That there hath past away a glory from the earth.*[1]

No, the glory hasn't passed away from the earth; what has been lost is the adult's ability to feel, to sense, to trust. Somewhere along the line, the potential of the child has withered into the weakness of the adult. Yet — yet the *potens* remains. It is possible, Jesus has taught us, to be "born again," to release anew that inner strength; this time the birth is not of "flesh and blood" but of water and spirit.

The reborn child has a new parent, and

to all who received him, to those who believed in his name, he gave the right to become children of God—children born not of natural descent, nor of human decision or a husband's will, but born of God (John 1:12).

The first birth was biological, resulting from union of male and female; the second is spiritual, when Spirit overwhelms spirit, and strength conquers weakness.

I See Trust

It's taken for granted, of course. Nick unconsciously accepts the breast from which he feeds, the arms that hold him secure, the hovering of parent and grandparent. He will trust until trust is violated. In the meantime, for him it's just there. He doesn't doubt. I, too, have taken this for granted. In fact, I didn't think of it for a while. The infant has no choice. Only later, in the maturing process (the terrible twos, or, as in Kyle's case earlier than two—I told you he is precocious), is trust withheld. The maturing personality doubts, prefers to do it himself, experiments (endlessly) with his new-found "No." Independence appears, not yet sure of itself yet sure it can do it better than the bumbling parent. We applaud this sign of maturation. And we fear.

While writing this chapter, I flew to Indianapolis for a meeting of The Christians' Hour board. We took a break in the long day's deliberations to have a meal together at a local seafood restaurant. The evening was a memorable one for me as our friendly, accommodating, but not too well coordinated waitress dumped a bowl of tartar sauce on me. I was wearing my brand new sweater which, fortunately, was almost the shade of tartar sauce, so the damage was minimal. She was most apologetic and hastened to get additional napkins to clean the sweater, then returned to her task of clearing the table. This positioned her perfectly for her next act, tipping over my full coffee cup, which took care of my slacks. It was a performance deserving a scene in a Marx brothers movie.

The evening wasn't a total disaster, though. As we ate, I had been eyeing a young family at a nearby table, Mom and Dad and three tow-headed preschoolers, one a baby in her mother's arms. If ever there was a picture of an ideal American family, I was watching it. On the airplane I had been scribbling some notes for this chapter, so thoughts of babies and children were still dancing in my mind. I stared at the baby, so content in her mother's arms, the personification of helplessness, yet enjoying a strength not her own, protected by her tender mother's caresses, her father's watchful eye, and even her older brothers' protectiveness. There she was, surrounded by her guardian angels, totally oblivious to the strength that protected her.

Garrison Keillor writes of the evening Sue Niles disparages her parents at dinner as "the most boring, odious, disgusting people" she ever saw. She hates them. Instead of shocking the old folks, she must have been the startled one when they agreed with her. In fact, they have their own announcement to make. Her mother speaks:

> It's taken us a long time to face up to this, but you two are just not the right children for us. It's not your fault, any more than it is ours. Please try to understand. You're a constant source of aggravation—the mess, the endless clutter and noise and confusion and hostility. It makes for a stifling atmosphere for mine and Ron's relationship. We're all the time being parents, we don't have time to grow. I choose not to accept that.

Ron takes Nancy's hand and picks up the narrative: "I don't know if our marriage can survive your adolescence," he said. "We've come to a decision. We have to do what's best for us. We're going to sell you."[2]

Keillor's humor is delightful. But his little story wouldn't be funny if it were true. Selling the children is something good parents don't consider, ever, for any reason! They die first. They may even feel like the mother who, when she was asked, "Would you have children if you had to do it over again?" answered, "Sure, but not the same ones." They may identify with her, but they wouldn't act on their feeling because love won't allow it. That's why loved children can trust.

Such, then, are some of the traits this musing grandfather observes in God's latest gift to our family. He can't keep Psalm 139 out of his head:

> For you created my inmost being; you knit me together in my mother's womb. I praise you because I am fearfully and wonderfully made; your works are wonderful, I know that full well (verses 13, 14).

I am in awe as I look at this God-built creation I call, with laughable pride of ownership, my grandson—as if I had anything to do with putting him together. In a more reflective mood, I call him God's baby, for it was He who knitted him together and produced someone "fearfully and wonderfully made." His mother, who loved him before she knew him, had already begun to protect him. Tortured by allergies during her pregnancy, she took no antihistamines lest he be harmed. Never a smoker, no power on earth could have persuaded her to start. No alcohol, no aspirin, nothing that could harm the baby went into her system. She ate balanced meals and followed the doctor's regimen. Already she was treating God's gift to her with respect.

Meanwhile the grandfather is thinking of the whole birthing process, from conception to delivery, as an excellent spiritual illustration. Of course, as with all his deepest thoughts, he is only thinking another's thoughts after him, in this case the Psalmist's who, without having ever seen my grandsons, knows their essence. "My frame was not hidden from you when I was made in the secret place. When I was woven together in the depths of the earth, your eyes saw my unformed body" (Psalm 139:15, 16). Elsewhere, John, writing as a very old man, calls the Christians to whom he writes his "dear children" (1 John 2:1, 12, 18, etc.). His is the language of age to any younger person; it is also an acknowledgment of the perpetual childhood of the Christian who has deliberately started over, called not to be wise and stately but humble and childlike.

"How great is the love the Father has lavished on us, that we should be called children of God! And that is what we are!" (1 John 3:1). We are not to be like children in all things, of course; there is a difference between "childlike" and "childish." Paul makes the distinction clear in 1 Corinthians 14:20: "Brothers, stop thinking like children. In regard to evil be infants, but in your thinking be adults." Innocent children can see and know what their elders have tuned out:

> At that time Jesus, full of joy through the Holy Spirit, said, "I praise you, Father, Lord of heaven and earth, because you have hidden these things from the wise and learned, and revealed them to little children. Yes, Father, for this was your good pleasure" (Luke 10:21).

Thus ends the grandfather's meditation. He leaves his grandsons—but only for a while—a little in awe of the strength of children.

They used to seem so weak.

Notes

[1]William Wordsworth, "Intimations of Immortality from Recollections of Early Childhood."

[2]Garrison Keillor, *We Are Still Married* (New York: Viking, 1989), p. 55.

3

When I Am Weak, Then I Am Strong

Luke 2:41-52

We don't know much about Jesus between birth and adulthood. The only tantalizing glimpse we are given is of His presentation in the temple. (When He was bar mitzvahed, we would say today.) One convincing proof of the Bible's reliability is the absence of miracle stories about the child Jesus. (There are plenty of them in apocryphal sources.) As far as the Gospel writers were concerned, Jesus' childhood was typical of a Jewish boy of His time; only one anecdote from this period was worthy of record.

As a young person, I tried to imagine what it must have been like for Jesus, astounding the teachers, a prodigy among the professors. While there is nothing miraculous about the event, still no twelve-year-old I've known (including and especially myself) could command adult attention as Jesus does here.

What I didn't know then, however, was that all adults are well advised to listen to the words of the young. These days I'm more sensitive to this truth than I used to be, more willing, as I mentioned in the last chapter, to let the grandchildren teach me.

My awareness has been heightened because a few weeks ago I heard a couple of California educators speak about the state's children and young people. They both asserted that never in history has there been anything like the melding and mixing of so many different ethnic groups speaking so many languages living in one geographical location (the greater Los Angeles area). The challenge for public and private education is nearly overwhelming, the job made even more difficult by the fact that today's educators are strangers to the world today's children are growing up in. The speakers repeatedly admonished us to listen carefully to what the children teach us about their world; otherwise we will never get them to listen to what we think they should know about ours. Children seem so young, so ignorant and fragile. But only they can initiate us into the mysteries of their world. They hold the key to an educator's success. They only seem weak.

While listening to the California educators, I recalled a day a decade ago when I told our three teenagers I didn't know whether I could continue to be a pastor after they left home. "I'll lose touch," I told them. And I have. The world of today's teenagers is alien to me. They speak a different language, eat stuff my body will not accept without complaint, and enjoy music more for its volume and assault on the body than for its tune or lyrics. It's a strange world they live in.

Yet each year convinces me further that I must listen to them. They are where "it's happenin'." They are "what's happenin'." Every year I grow biologically weaker, they grow stronger. My generation appears to wield the power. Only apparently, and only for a while. We must listen to them, or before long they will dismiss us from the scene.

I'm grateful I still have some young friends. They teach me the tricks of survival in their world. Without their tutoring, I'd spend too much time in the company of the learned and important and would probably congratulate myself on being one of the strong ones.

My doctoral studies (as I was learning "more and more about less and less") taught me that a formal education both qualifies and disqualifies a person. The more intently I pursued my "book learning," the more inept I grew in certain manual skills and activities and the more I withdrew from a social life. Joy and I were able to laugh about it, saying that I had temporarily dropped out and Joy had to take over the living for both of us. It was only partially a joke. I was too busy doing important things, thinking important thoughts, writing important papers, hobnobbing with important professors and fellow students, to be bothered by little things.

Thankfully, we had three small children in those days; they kept me real. I made it a practice to return from the library each afternoon in time to watch *Mr. Rogers* and *Sesame Street* with them, and then eat and play together (sometimes at the same time, to their mother's dismay). And they taught me.

They saved me from becoming a mere academician. They kept alive my sense of humor and my need to earn money to feed them, and they fed my emotions. They restored my balance. I earned the Ph.D. They earned my eternal gratitude.

Only after so nearly losing my equilibrium did I come to appreciate fully Luke 2:52 as a formula for a balanced life.

"And Jesus grew in wisdom and stature, and in favor with God and men."

The Stature of a Child

Let me disturb the order of the formula for a moment. The Greek word for stature, *helikia*, merely observes that Jesus' physical growth was appropriate to his age.

We have precious little control over the size or shape of our bodies, of course, although we have developed some quirky attitudes about them. Our culture equates big with better, even when talking about children. We say that Joey, short for his age group, is "cute," but we brag more about Chuck who is three inches taller than the charts predict for his age. We expect more of larger children, which may give taller ones an edge on IQ tests,[1] and we definitely hope for tall children. (Some parents even seek physicians' help to force up the height of their average-sized children.)

We don't change our tune, either, when they grow up. Our society pays tall people better than short people, definitely prefers tall people as corporate CEOs, and teases shorties mercilessly. Ziggy's doctor tells him, "The test results are in. . . . You're too short."[2] Senator Snort tells his public relations agent, "I'm paying you a lot of money to improve my image, Figby! For starters, I want to be taller!"[3]

Occasionally someone strikes back, as did Francis Bacon clear back in the seventeenth century: "Wise nature did never put her precious jewels into a garret four stories high: and therefore . . . exceeding tall men had ever very empty heads." But then, who today has heard of Francis Bacon? We know Albert Einstein was short and Mohandas Gandhi was shorter, but we still hope our sons will incline more favorably toward Arnold Schwarzenegger or Sylvester Stallone.

Consciously or subconsciously, then, we equate size with strength: bigger is stronger and better, smaller is weaker and more pitiful.

We are consciously or subconsciously wrong.

You may accuse me of being a little defensive on this subject, but I hope I'm not. Having come from a long line of decidedly diminutive but happy people, and having spent several years being not only short but also young, I can testify that when I was weak, then I was strong.

When I was a young man in the ministry, it must have been pretty hard for people to take me seriously. Those who knew me did, and our church grew in spite of (or because of) my physical limitations. (In Christ there is neither tall nor short!) Away from the church, though, is where I experienced the real strength in my weakness.

Because I was young, inexperienced, and insignificant looking, people didn't take me seriously. They were themselves around me, for better or for worse (often for worse). Nobody called me sir or opened doors for me or performed any of the other myriad maneuvers of etiquette. In other words, they felt no need to be on their best behavior.

They were to me as most adults are to children: they treated me as if I didn't exist, or existing, didn't matter. As a result, I was a shrewder judge of character then. Unfortunately, while I am no taller than ever, I am grayer and more encumbered with titles. In my official and social roles now, people are polite and I have difficulty seeing through the veneer. Now that I am stronger, I am weaker.

Jesus didn't have my particular inconvenience, but He knew what it was to grow up as a seemingly insignificant child of a not-very-important family in a little-regarded town in a despised nation at the very edge of the powerful Roman empire. What an advantage. Possessing so many weaknesses, He could become very strong.

The Wisdom of a Child

We move on to the weightier part of the formula. "Jesus grew in wisdom." Luke chooses *wisdom* rather than *knowledge*, a surprising selection. When do we ever hear an adult speak of a child's wisdom? We consider children as smart, or as knowing a lot for their age, but only a most exceptional child would we call wise.

Once again, we adults may not be as clever as we think. Every time I'm with children for a while, they intimidate me. As a matter of fact, I've made it a policy not to try to answer questions from children. Only from adults. The children's are too hard. They haven't learned our trick of ruling out whole blocks of reality when new data challenge the old. They insist on answers to the unanswerable.

When Jesus finished speaking the words of the Sermon on the Mount, "the crowds were amazed" (Matthew 7:28). No wonder. The speaker was already amazing teachers when He was twelve. Throughout His brief ministry, He not only astounded but disturbed. Religious leaders took exception to His unconventional teaching. That, too, is predictable. Even His parents didn't understand Him: "Why have you treated us like this?" their exasperation demanded to know.

The brief conversation isn't really a dialogue. Parents and son talk past one another. "Your father and I have been anxiously searching for you." Hurt and perhaps anger and certainly misunderstanding color their words.

"Why were you searching for me?" He asks. Surely they knew, "I had to be in my Father's house."

The clash was inevitable. The Son's business was not the parents'. Neither was His world their world. Did they think Him wise or merely willful? Luke calls Him "obedient to them" in the very next sentence, perhaps to assure his readers that something far more important than adolescent rebellion was at stake here.

How many moments of my parenting days would I live over if I could, moments when I dealt severely with children I believed were being disobedient when really they were merely expressing a wisdom not my own, acting on conclusions logically drawn from the data of their quite different world. I didn't call it wisdom. I called it willfulness, and I determined to bend them into my world, one for which God never destined nor fitted them.

Mary treasured her memories of Jesus in those years and must have told them later. This one Luke picked up to include in his account of Jesus' life. He probably selected it because he perceived it to be significant, perhaps even *the* pivotal point in Jesus' maturation. Here He takes His stand: He must dwell in His Father's "house," not Joseph's. The wisdom of this world could never become His; His would be an unworldly, a "godly" wisdom. Only as He adhered to it could He be strong—with a strength this world calls weakness.

Robert Fulghum made the best seller lists with his book, *All I Really Need to Know I Learned in Kindergarten*.[4] I wish we knew the age of the readers. My guess is it has enjoyed more popularity among us old-timers than among younger adults, who are not as far removed from kindergarten. With years and experience and heartache comes a longing for the unworldly wisdom of childhood. We become more religious in later life. This world's wisdom cloys after a while. What used to be sweet now almost sickens. Our hearts turn back with Fulghum's, away from "the top of the graduate-school mountain" (where in such rarified air wisdom seldom grows) to the "sandpile at Sunday school," where we learned these important things:

Share everything.
Play fair.
Don't hit people.
Put things back where you found them.
Clean up your own mess.
Don't take things that aren't yours.
Say you're sorry when you hurt somebody.
Wash your hands before you eat.
Flush.
Warm cookies and cold milk are good for you.
Live a balanced life—learn some and think some and draw and paint and sing and dance and play and work every day some.
Take a nap every afternoon.
When you go out into the world, watch out for traffic, hold hands, and stick together.
Be aware of wonder. Remember the little seed in the Styrofoam cup: The roots go down and the plant goes up and nobody really knows how or why, but we are all like that.

> Goldfish and hamsters and white mice and even the little seed in the Styrofoam cup—they all die. So do we.
>
> And then remember the Dick-and-Jane books and the first word you learned—the biggest word of all—LOOK.

Not adult "conventional wisdom," but truth.

My good friend Russ Blowers, a minister in Indianapolis, Indiana, was inspired by Fulghum to add up his own list of "the basic things I learned in White Cottage, Ohio, as a little boy."

> God is bigger than you can imagine. He's everywhere and can do anything, and He sees what you're doing.
>
> Hard work is good for you.
>
> When somebody dies you take food in.
>
> Dads are people who come home every day at 5. Mothers hold your head when you throw up.
>
> Two or three presents are enough at Christmas.
>
> It's OK to cry at funerals.
>
> All you need to get a good education is a teacher who likes to teach and has something to teach, an average brain, and two parents who encourage you.
>
> Old people are often ignored and neglected but they have a lot to offer.
>
> You're in big trouble if you marry the wrong person.
>
> Neighbors are put there in case you need to borrow a cup of sugar.
>
> Just because you, the fat boy, and the skinny girl were the last to be chosen for the team at recess doesn't mean you're not as good as everyone else.
>
> Things are going to get better.[5]

Both of these good lists belong in a book whose theme is, "When I am weak, then I am strong," because a corollary is the theme of this chapter: "When I seem wise, then I am foolish; when I seem foolish, it may be because in that instance I am acting wisely."

The apostle Paul speaks to this paradox in a letter to some very proud Christians in Corinth. They think themselves smart, moral, super spiritual, and highly gifted. Judged by God's standards, however, they seem to Paul to be foolish, immoral, worldly, and possessing in abundance every gift but the most important one, love. He doesn't have much use for their brand of worldly wisdom.

> God chose the foolish things of the world to shame the wise; God chose the weak things of the world to shame the strong. He chose the lowly things of this world and the despised things — and the things that are not — to nullify the things that are, so that no one may boast before him (1 Corinthians 1:27-29).

Paul finds strength in weakness, wisdom in foolishness, and real greatness in apparent lowliness. He himself is an example of personal weakness infused with God's power. To the world, Paul seems a nobody speaking nonsense. But because his message is God's and his power is the Spirit's, he is to the contrary an important somebody teaching some things even more important.

> I came to you in weakness and fear, and with much trembling. My message and my preaching were not with wise and persuasive words, but with a demonstration of the Spirit's power, so that your faith might not rest on men's wisdom, but on God's power.
>
> We do, however, speak a *message of wisdom* among the mature, but not the wisdom of this age or of the rulers of this age, who are coming to nothing. No, we speak of *God's secret wisdom*, a wisdom that has been hidden and that God destined for our glory before time began (1 Corinthians 2:3-7, italics mine).

As I said, everyone should heed Paul's message, since it is God-sent. Everyone should, but not everyone will.

This is what we speak, not in words taught us by human wisdom but in words taught by the Spirit, expressing spiritual truths in spiritual words. The man without the Spirit does not accept the things that come from the Spirit of God, for they are foolishness to him, and he cannot understand them, because they are spiritually discerned (1 Corinthians 2:13, 14).

Paul's contrast of worldly and spiritual wisdom makes one think of Jesus' prayer: "I praise you, Father, Lord of heaven and earth, because you have hidden these things from the wise and learned, and revealed them to little children" (Matthew 11:25, 26).

A child knows what Jesus taught His parents, that He must be in His Father's house, doing His Father's business.

The adolescent prefers to do things his own way, for his own purposes.

The adult, caught up in egocentric pursuits, becomes blind and deaf to the work of his Father, and stumbles into foolishness.

Thus Jesus calls us to learn again the wisdom of the child.

The Favor a Child Enjoys

The formula sounds simple, doesn't it? ". . . in favor with God and men." On the one hand, it is, as Jesus' great commandments:

"Love the Lord your God with all your heart and with all your soul and with all your mind." This is the first and greatest commandment. And the second is like it: "Love your neighbor as yourself" (Matthew 22:37-39).

These are the great inseparables.

To love God and hate, or even disregard, human beings is not to love God.

To find favor with God is to do favors for persons. To be acceptedly wise to God is to act wisely toward humanity.

You can't separate spiritual and social wisdom. Favor with God and favor with man are one, as love of God and man are one.

Yet Luke's formula doesn't reveal the whole story. Jesus found favor with God, all right, of that the record is clear. But He didn't always find favor with men. Had He been able to, no cross would have put a stop to His ministry. He went about doing favors for men and women, that's true, but He also got himself into a great deal of trouble with them. He still does.

Luke could more accurately have said, "and in favor with God and *certain* men (and women)." Some couldn't (and can't) stand Him: the worldly wise, the self-righteous, the controller, the manipulator, the greedy, the me-firster, the racist, the self-satisfied, the cruelly ambitious, the snobbishly intellectual.

With whom then did (and does) He find favor?

The poor, who believe He cares and helps.

The outsiders, who sense His acceptance.

The seeking, who trust His patience with their doubts.

The needy, who find their relief in Him.

The rejected, who know He looks on the heart and not the surface.

The hungry and thirsty for genuine righteousness, who find its source in Him.

The skeptical, who aren't fooled by what this world calls wisdom and are relieved to discover something truer and surer in Him.

The merciful, who appreciate someone even more merciful than they.

What this means is that, like Jesus, His disciples are forced to choose whose favor we wish to curry. When you try to please everybody, you please nobody; in fact, you merely look—because you are—foolish. But if you believe the essence of wisdom is pleasing God, you will enjoy the favor of the people He favors.

And you will enjoy strength beyond your weakness.

Notes

[1]*Psychology Today*, March, 1987, p. 14.

[2]Tom Wilson, *Ziggy*, © 1985, Universal Press Syndicate.

[3]Rick Gager, *Grin and Bear It*, © 1988, North American Syndicate, Inc.

[4]From *All I Really Need to Know I Learned in Kindergarten*, by Robert Fulghum, © 1986, 1988 by Robert Fulghum. Reprinted by permission of Villard Books, a division of Random House, Inc.

[5]Russ Blowers, "Minister's Memo," *The Ninety-First Edition*, April, 1990, p. 2.

4

WHEN I AM POOR,
THEN I AM RICH

Matthew 5:1-12

We were riding together in our church van from Mesa to Fullerton, at least a seven-hour drive. Mike, Judy, Barbara, Mark C., and Mark H.—pastors and directors of our Arizona church—were on their way to a conference at Buena Park, close enough to our college in Fullerton that they could drop me off.

I had taken along a laptop computer so I could work on this book as we traveled. They asked the theme of the book. "With a strength not my own," I told them. Then I asked, "When have you felt your strongest?"

Barb, mother of two little boys (and pregnant with her third child) quickly answered, "When I gave birth."

Mark H. recalled how strong he felt the day he was married.

For Mark C., it was on the athletic field, when he knew "no one could beat me—no way could I lose."

Judy, the mother of three grown children said, "When I know that other people are dependent on me to come through, and I know I have to do it; my back's against the wall."

While Mike was thinking through his response, I asked the second question: "When have you felt your weakest?"

Immediately Mark H. asked, "Could it be the same event?" For him, becoming married made him feel strong and weak all at once.

Barb agreed. Having felt her strongest in giving birth, she now added that having a baby made her feel her weakest as well.

Mark C. mentioned something that happened the previous Sunday, when a woman told him, "Tomorrow they are taking my dad off the respirator and he will die." What could he say? How could he comfort her?

Judy said she felt her most hopeless in a foreign country when she couldn't understand the language. "You are at the mercy of everybody else."

I quickly agreed. Never have I felt more insufficient — nor more foolish — than when having a little child pick the correct coins out of my hand because I didn't know the currency nor the language of his people.

Mike agreed with Mark H. and Barb that he has felt both his strongest and his weakest in the same kind of situation. "When a person comes to me needing help of some kind, and I have been prepared and had something to offer, I feel strong. But many times they are going through things I can't relate to or I can't come up with what they need to hear. Then I feel my weakest."

Barb added that when she feels God's presence, she feels her strongest and her weakest all at once.

Mark H. then thought of another event. When he was ordained into the Christian ministry and the charge was delivered to him, he felt weakness and strength.

Our conversation continued for many miles. We were fascinated by it. "When you are stressed out emotionally," someone mused, "all your decisions are weak because you are worn down."

Judy, on a study sabbatical from the church, spoke for all students when she said, "I find a lot of weak moments in math class."

Mark C. added that, for him, one of the weakest-strongest experiences is preaching.

Barb, the newest Christian in the group, gave her testimony. "It's a difference of whom you rely on. Before [becoming a Christian], I relied on the quick fix: partying, buying something, going out drinking. Now, the down times don't last as long. You pull yourself out with a long term fix—the Christian life. It's like runners hitting the wall. All of a sudden you go over the wall, and it just takes over. You don't have to make decisions anymore. It just takes over."

Other than myself, Judy has been a Christian the longest in the group. "If I didn't have Christ, I'd be in an entirely different place physically, mentally, and in every way. I would probably not be with my family. In the early years of my marriage, when it was tough, I'd have bailed out. I've often wondered what I would have been. So being Christian, a lot of things have happened to me that happen to non-Christians, but I don't think I've ever felt the hopelessness others experience. I never doubt that He's there. I've never thought that things shouldn't happen to me. I never doubted that He cares."

Mark H. recalled "things that have *not* happened." He was spared much, he feels, because people prayed for him. "I am human, tempted like everyone else, yet there's a strength that's God's grace." He spoke of a man in his home church who prayed every Sunday for the youth of the church. "God honored that prayer in my life."

Mark C. spoke of temptations he's been able to avoid. "Knowing I have 'a strength not my own' on my side, there's nothing I can't handle. I've never felt overwhelmed by temptations that I couldn't handle or I'd have to give in to." He was thinking of parties, especially. "They weren't something I *had* to do."

Mike gave thanks for "personal disciplines, for being able to develop areas I know on my own I wouldn't have been able to do." He also expressed appreciation for "the power of prayer that's available and the strength that I receive through obvious answered prayer." He said he feels weakest when he realizes he hasn't accessed that free gift of prayer.

The hours seemed like minutes as we explored this subject. What surprised us was the difficulty we had separating weakness from strength. All of us were impressed by how little we relied on our own power (and what puny results we achieved when we did) and how often, when we were inadequate, we accomplished results beyond our ability. God provided the strength not our own.

Remembering experiences of feeling strong and weak at the same time helps us understand Jesus' famous Beatitudes. These often paradoxical remarks are among His most difficult for a newcomer to Christianity to understand. How can it be a blessing to be poor in spirit or in mourning or meek or persecuted? What does He mean? He means there's strength in weakness.

"Blessed are the poor in spirit, for theirs is the kingdom of heaven."

Luke quotes Jesus even more tersely: "Blessed are you who are poor, for yours is the kingdom of God" (Luke 6:20). Whether He is speaking of material or spiritual poverty, the blessing is the same. The poor are in a position to receive. Further, they aren't so tempted to demand or put on airs. To do so only makes them look ridiculous, since they will inevitably be found out. Their pretense will shut out potential gifts or any potential donor naturally concluding they are already quite satisfied.

But when you are admittedly poor, humility becomes you. You recognize your limitations, whether financial or social or psychological. You find it easier to submit to Another, who has what you are lacking.

To submit. That's the word to remember, the key to marital harmony—"Submit to one another out of reverence for Christ" (Ephesians 5:21)—and to harmony in civil (Romans 13:1; Titus 3:1; 1 Peter 2:13), church (1 Corinthians 16:15, 16), and spiritual life in general (Hebrews 12:9; James 4:7).

The alternative to submission is rebellion. Defiance keeps us from acknowledging God's superiority. Rebellion separates us from the source of strength and grace. By asserting our self-sufficiency, we deny ourselves access to divine power. When we are strong, then we are weak.

Long ago, I learned from my counselees that there is no greater human need than to learn to submit. The submissive, the poor in spirit, open themselves up to the Lord's blessings.

"Blessed are those who mourn, for they will be comforted."

You never feel weaker than you do when you are mourning. If you could bring her back, you would. In fact, you did everything within your power to prevent her dying. You prayed, you argued with the doctors, you went without sleep, you took time off work, you soothed her, you were there. But you weren't enough. She died anyway.

Yet Jesus calls your condition "blessed"! How could He?

Because, in a very real sense, you are already experiencing something positive. Suppose you didn't hurt? Suppose you didn't care? Even worse, suppose you couldn't?

When my stepfather died, almost our whole family mourned. He and my mother had been married twenty-five years. Although at first we children viewed the marriage with skepticism (perhaps even disfavor), Jack proved an exceptionally good man, caring for Mother and embracing us kids in his love even though he already had a large family of his own.

So when he died, after lingering for several days in the intensive care unit, we grieved. Most of us, that is. Mother didn't. In fact, after the funeral, she never mentioned his name again.

She didn't dislike him. She just didn't miss him. He was already forgotten.

Mother was sinking into Alzheimer's Disease. She didn't have the capacity to mourn. She was sick.

Blessed are you when you feel the loss of a loved one, when you can remember shared experiences, when you can break out of your circle of selfishness to sense another's presence or absence.

Blessed are the sensitive.

Blessed are those who care enough to feel diminished by the departure of another.

Blessed are those who admit their need of others.

Blessed are those who, knowing their weakness when alone, draw strength from their bond with others stronger than they.

They shall be comforted. Comforted by the love and presence of others, by the love and presence of God. Comforted by their hope of eternal life.

"Blessed are the meek, for they will inherit the earth."

One always thinks of Moses, who was *very* meek, "above all the men which were upon the face of the earth" (Numbers 12:3, KJV). To mention Moses is to confirm that, contrary to popular opinion, meekness cannot mean weakness. No weakling could have slain the Egyptian with his bare hands; no weakling could have inspired a nation of people to follow him in the wilderness for forty years.

What, then, does the Bible mean by "meek"?

A few more Scriptures may enlighten us. An exasperated apostle Paul appeals to his critics in the Corinthian church "by the *meekness* and gentleness of Christ " (2 Corinthians 10:1). This helps. Our mental picture of Jesus is of one physically strong (with a carpenter's hands), psychologically stable, with a charismatic personality and the ability to perform superhuman miracles, but without arrogance or pretense. Quite simply, He was who He seemed to be. He had nothing to prove. More importantly, He was directed by a strong sense of purpose. He had a mission to fulfill, one He recognized while still a youth ("Didn't you know I had to be in my Father's house?" Luke 2:49) and from which He never wavered. ("Yet not as I will, but as you will" Matthew 26:39.)

Further, meekness (translated as *humility* in the New International Version) is an attribute of the mature Christian. "Be completely humble and gentle; be patient, bearing with one another in love" (Ephesians 4:2). Paul uses the imperative mood for the verb. It's an order. He's paying us a compliment, actually, of assuming our ability to do so. You don't say to a doormat or Caspar Milquetoast, "Be humble." To such a person you give a different order: "Stand up. Be a man. Assert yourself!"

Jesus draws on Psalm 37:10 and 11 in this Beatitude.

A little while, and the wicked will be no more;
    though you look for them, they will not be found.
But the meek will inherit the land
    and enjoy great peace.

The contest is not between meekness and strength, but meekness and wickedness. Though they may seem to have the upper hand now, the wicked will not inherit the earth.

"They are like chaff that the wind blows away. . . . For the Lord watches over the way of the righteous, but the way of the wicked will perish" (Psalm 1:4, 6).

In the first Beatitude, Jesus is speaking of now. To the poor in spirit, "theirs is [present tense, now] the kingdom of heaven." In the third, the meek *will* [future tense] inherit the earth." The meek appear to be the losers; they aren't the power brokers, the movers and shakers, the obvious winners in this world's rat race. (But that's not all bad. Somebody said the problem with the rat race is that, even if you win, you're still a rat.) They take the lesser role; they are pulled by a higher vision, a prior obedience. True to their calling, they put up with inconvenience now, but the time is coming when they will receive all that has been promised. They'll inherit the earth.

There's also a sense in which the meek are already enjoying their inheritance. Since they don't feel the need to control or own anything, they take pleasure in other people's enjoyment of their possessions. And, since they know this is their Father's world, they glory in all that is His, the grandeur of the mountains, the glory of the sunrises and sunsets, the precision of His architecture, the mystery of His atoms.

They have already come into some of their inheritance, having been given His Spirit as "a deposit guaranteeing our inheritance until the redemption of those who are God's possession" (Ephesians 1:14). Having already been given so much, and having been promised so much more, the meek tolerate their temporary inconveniences without complaint.

"Blessed are those who hunger and thirst for righteousness, for they will be filled."

When we were getting ready to build our new church building, the planning committee often used a certain phrase. It first came up when we were preparing to select a contractor. We hoped bids for the job would come in low; they would, we said, if the contractors were "hungry enough." Since Arizona was growing rapidly at that time, the contractors were busy. That was not a good sign. They would not be "hungry enough" for our business.

When we were under construction, we sometimes had to call subcontractors back to repair some shoddy work. They had so much other business they didn't worry much about pleasing us. They weren't hungry enough.

It's an instructive use of the metaphor, isn't it? Jesus makes exactly the same application. He is talking about people for whom righteousness is a passion, a hunger—like that of a starving person seeking food, a hungry laborer seeking work. People who care that much about being right with God as well as with people will achieve their goal.

They seem weak, don't they? Certainly they can't boast of having or being all they need. They want more. The good news is that more of what they want is available. They will be satisfied.

Jesus may have Isaiah 55:1 and 2 in mind:

Come, all you who are thirsty,
   come to the waters;
and you who have no money,
   come, buy and eat!
Come, buy wine and milk
   without money and without cost.
Why spend money on what is not bread,
   and your labor on what does not satisfy?
Listen, listen to me, and eat what is good,
   and your soul will delight in the richest of fare.

This passion for righteousness is not sated by observing rites or performing sacrifices; instead, it is found in relationships. Jesus invites the thirsty to quench their longing when, on the last day of the Feast of Tabernacles in Jerusalem, He announces, "If a man is thirsty, let him come to me and drink. Whoever believes in me, as the Scripture has said, streams of living water will flow from within him" (John 7:37, 38).

John says Jesus is speaking of the Holy Spirit, the Lord's abiding presence. Jesus' promise here is twofold: first, the thirsty person will be satisfied; second, he'll receive so much it will in turn flow out from him, thus blessing others. In this one promise, the two elements of righteousness are given: being right with God and with other people.

"Blessed are the merciful, for they will be shown mercy."

When I asked my traveling companions what they thought this Beatitude meant, one of them blurted out the old adage, "What goes around comes around."

Then another immediately pointed out that it didn't work this way with Jesus. No one was ever more merciful than He; yet His efforts were rewarded by a crucifixion. What went around didn't come around.

Is Jesus then once again pointing beyond life to an eternal reward? Undoubtedly. But He is also repeating something He taught elsewhere in a little different language.

After teaching His disciples the Model Prayer, which includes the petition, "Forgive us our debts, as we also have forgiven our debtors," He warns of the implications of this request "For if you forgive men when they sin against you, your heavenly Father will also forgive you. But if you do not forgive men their sins, your Father will not forgive your sins" (Matthew 6:12, 14, 15).

The subject of mercy and forgiveness must have come up often among Jesus' disciples, probably because they had as much trouble with this teaching as we have. Once Peter asked Jesus how many times a person had to forgive, as many as seven? At least eleven times more than that, Jesus answered. Then, lest Peter should underestimate the gravity of an unforgiving attitude, Jesus told about an unmerciful servant who, having been forgiven, refused to be equally merciful (Matthew 18:21-35).

"In anger his master turned him over to the jailers . . . until he should pay back all he owed."

Then Jesus adds the moral of the story: "This is how my heavenly Father will treat each of you unless you forgive your brother from your heart."

Jesus' parable is all the explanation this Beatitude requires. The Lord has blotted out our sins. That's mercy.

What we have received, we give.

What we then give, we shall receive.

"Blessed are the pure in heart, for they will see God."

You see what you look for. Persons who say they really want to see God, and mean it, will see Him. He will not withhold himself from anyone who diligently seeks Him.

How much do you want to see God? As much as Paul? "May I never boast except in the cross of our Lord Jesus Christ, through which the world has been crucified to me, and I to the world" (Galatians 6:14).

Our phrase "dead to the world" takes on new meaning in light of Jesus' cross, doesn't it? When we have been "buried with him through baptism into death in order that, just as Christ was raised from the dead through the glory of the Father, we too may live a new life" (Romans 6:4), we are indeed dead to the world. It doesn't have power to pull us away from God anymore. We have pledged a new allegiance.

Purity of heart, as Soren Kierkegaard put it so long ago, is "to will one thing." That one thing is, indeed, to see God.

We aren't talking about wishful thinking here, though. As Washington Irving said, "Great minds have purposes; others have wishes." Wishing won't make it happen. Wanting to see God with such earnestness that nothing else compares, however, does.

When Paul charges Timothy to "keep yourself pure" (1 Timothy 5:22), he means for the younger man to refrain from sinful pursuits and to remember he has been ordained ("set apart," "made holy") to one purpose. He must now "will one thing."

John places the reason for purity in the future:

> Dear friends, now we are children of God, and what we will be has not yet been made known. But we know that when he appears, we shall be like him, for we shall see him as he is. Everyone who has this hope in him purifies himself, just as he is pure (1 John 3:2, 3).

So we focus our attention and our lives on one thing, believing He will reward that commitment.

"Blessed are the peacemakers, for they will be called sons of God."

They will wear the name of the Son, the Prince of Peace, who established peace between human beings (Ephesians 2:11-22) and between God and those who accept His grace (Romans 5:1).

Jesus is quite specific in this Beatitude. The blessing is for the peaceMAKER. Being a peace lover isn't good enough. The frazzled parent or harried spouse who just "wants a little peace and quiet around here" won't get it. This is not a Beatitude for the passive or timid or cowardly.

Jesus *made* peace, but it cost Him His life to do it. No one could accuse Him of passivity or timidity or cowardliness. He took on the chief disturbers of the peace in His day, yet without compromise to His principles. And when His enemies determined to kill Him to get Him out of the way, He didn't get even with them. Instead, He allowed himself to be condemned and crucified in order to protect the truth He came to teach.

How can we imitate Him? A brief moment in history can tell us. At the Paris Peace Conference in 1919, France's Premier Clemenceau insulted Woodrow Wilson. Losing his temper, he told the American President, who was trying to effect a lasting peace in the aftermath of World War I, "You talk like Jesus Christ!" Then he said to the assembled heads of state, "Gentlemen, I have heard much talk here about a permanent peace. You say you want a peace to end all wars. I would like to know whether you mean that." When they all nodded, Clemenceau delivered the telling blow, "If we want to give up war, we must give up our empires." Lest they miss his point, he became brutally specific. "You, Mr. Lloyd George [of England], will have to come up out of India. We French will have to come out of North Africa.

And you Americans, Mr. President, will have to relinquish your dollar rights in the Philippines, Mexico, and Cuba. We the dominant powers will have to give up our empires, tear down our tariff walls, free our colonies, and open up the world."

That isn't what they had in mind, the leaders told him. Then Clemenceau banged his fist on the table and said, "Then you don't mean peace, you want war."[1]

You can't make peace on earth and build your empires at the same time. You give up one or the other.

You can't make peace at home that way, either. Peace exists where all parties work for the good of others.

Jesus made peace by suffering rather than making others suffer, by dying rather than killing, by forgiving instead of getting even.

Peace is made by replacing your swords and guns and threats you wield with a cross you carry.

"Blessed are those who are persecuted because of righteousness, for theirs is the kingdom of heaven. Blessed are you when people insult you, persecute you and falsely say all kinds of evil against you because of me."

It doesn't matter what you do, you'll be criticized for it. (Lyndon Johnson, who experienced more than his share of disapproval, once claimed that if one morning he walked on top of the water across the Potomac River, the headline that afternoon would read, "President Can't Swim."[2]) Realizing this simple truth early in my ministry was one of the most liberating thoughts I have entertained. It freed me to serve the Lord without fear. Since criticism is inevitable for anyone in leadership, I would accept the inevitable, but I would reserve for myself the right to choose what I would be criticized for.

Jesus' word is stronger: *persecuted*. Sometimes criticism almost feels like persecution. Some can easily be brushed off, like Ted Turner's labeling Christianity a "religion for losers"[3] or the anonymous wit who quipped, "He's a born-again Christian. The trouble is, he suffered brain damage during rebirth." Often it's much more serious. C. T. Studd, missionary in China in the 1880s, reported he couldn't venture outside without a volley of curses from his neighbors. Worldwide, things haven't improved since then. In fact, the twentieth century has been the century for persecution of Christians, the bloodiest period in all history for believers in Christ, averaging 300,000 Christian martyrdoms each year. According to David Barrett editor of the *World Christian Encyclopedia*, martyrdom is not an "outrageous exception, but a part of a surprisingly regular 2,000-year pattern where persecution and suffering are the normal lot of the body of Christ."[4]

Jesus foresaw the fate of His faithful. He encourages them in their times of trial by this simple reminder that they are not destined for success in this world or on this world's terms, but if they will remain faithful in their relationship with the Lord and in their mission on His behalf, they will indeed enjoy their home in His kingdom forever.

They only seem weak.

They are strong; they are the real survivors.

Notes

[1]J. Wallace Hamilton, *Serendipity* (Westwood, New Jersey: Fleming H. Revell Co., 1965).

[2]Quoted by Ronald Reagan in Hugh Sidey, "The Presidency," *Time*, December 28, 1987, p. 22.

[3]*Time*, May 14, 1990, p. 25.

[4]*Christianity Today*, March 19, 1990, p. 12.

5

How to Walk by Faith

Matthew 8:5-13

When I began this chapter, I intended to write about the centurion's servant. Unable to heal himself, he is the perfect illustration of weakness made strong by "a strength not its own." Here is our theme *in extremis*. Haven't you experienced a moment when someone else had to be strong FOR you? Or had so weak a faith another had to believe FOR you?

Often beside a hospital bed I've heard a patient confess, "I can't even pray."

"Don't worry," I've said while taking a hand. "Now it's our turn to pray for you."

As I said, my intention was to fix our attention on the patient, but the noble centurion deserves the closer study. What an unusual role reversal he undergoes here. A military man accustomed to acting from strength, he now can get what he wants only by admitting his weakness.

"I myself am a man under authority, with soldiers under me. I tell this one, 'Go,' and he goes; and that one, 'Come,' and he comes. I say to my servant, 'Do this,' and he does it" (Matthew 8:9).

His career has been built on power, and he has wielded it skillfully. His servant's terrible suffering, however, carries him beyond his authority. He can't order the sickness gone, the paralysis exorcised. The symbols of his rank strike no fear in the paralysis. His dependent's helplessness is matched by a feebleness of his own. He can huff and puff all he wants, but the disease will not yield, not

even to an officer of Rome. His meekness before the affliction parallels his humility before the Great Physician. He
knows his place. He may be an officer of the occupying
army and Jesus but an untitled commoner in the occupied territory, but these distinctions are meaningless now.

The centurion doesn't stand on ceremony. He has the
right to demand anything of Jesus, but he asks nothing
for himself. He pleads for his servant.

I can't help thinking of another great man who refused
to stand on ceremony. He, too, had more concern for his
cause than his rights.

Early in the War between the States, Union President
Abraham Lincoln, fearing that General Lee's Confederate
troops would storm Washington, visited the commander
of his Army of the Potomac, General George McClellan.
A cabinet member accompanied the President.

According to protocol, the President should have summoned his subordinate to the White House, but Lincoln
couldn't be bothered with the niceties of etiquette with a
war to conduct.

General McClellan was away when they arrived, so the
two men were seated. After an hour or so they heard his
voice in the hall and prepared to greet him, but instead of
entering their room, the general headed upstairs. Finally,
when another half hour had gone by, they dispatched a
servant to tell McClellan the President was still waiting.

The embarrassed servant returned to report McClellan
was too tired for a conference, so he had gone to bed.

Outside the house the cabinet member exploded,
demanding Lincoln immediately remove McClellan from
command. Lincoln's response is among his most quoted
lines: "There, there, I will hold McClellan's horse if only
he will bring us victories."

In that same humble spirit, the centurion pleads his
case. His faith and submissiveness captivate Jesus, and
His strength overcomes the servant's (and the servant's
master's) weakness.

We must look more closely at this remarkable officer who causes Jesus to marvel: "I tell you the truth, I have not found anyone in Israel with such great faith" (Matthew 8:10). From this centurion we can learn something of what it means to walk by faith and, in so doing, to turn weakness to strength.

One Who Walks by Faith Asks Instead of Orders

Our language depicts our condition. We "ask for help," we don't "tell for help." We may, if we are in a position of authority, order help sent—but, as we have seen, the sicker we are, the less position we are in to demand anything.

Mark McCormack, advisor of businessmen, believes most chairmen and CEO-level executives have learned what many people never learn: how to articulate these three hard-to-say phrases:

"I don't know."

"I need help."

"I was wrong."[1]

They are such simple words. What makes them so hard to utter? We stutter over them because they make us sound—well, you know, weak.

One's stumbling over them proves how weak he is. The truly knowledgeable are unafraid to admit what they don't know; the genuinely strong ask for help; the generally right can admit when they are wrong. (Oh, yes! We all know some "con" men who can feign ignorance or helplessness or repentance when they don't mean it—but I'm assuming that no "cons" will bother reading this book.)

My biggest frustration as an administrator surfaces here. I can tolerate almost any mistake by an employee, but how I long to hear, how I'll trust, how I'll promote someone who has the strength to confess, "I was wrong," or, "It was my mistake." I equally appreciate one who admits he doesn't know but wants to learn, and the one who is dependably competent but asks for help when it's needed.

The centurion's thoughtfulness is remarkable, his humility genuine. "Just say the word" (Matthew 8:8). That's enough. Jesus wouldn't need to go to his house.

His spirit is like that of actor Robert Young's little girl. Saying her prayers one evening, her list of "asks" grew so long she must have embarrassed herself. She suddenly stopped, paused, then finished in a small voice, "And now, dear God, is there anything I could do for you?"

We tend to pray more in the spirit of Huck Finn, whose failure in prayer causes him to abandon it altogether.

> Miss Watson she took me in the closet and prayed, but nothing come of it. She told me to pray every day, and whatever I asked for I would get it. But it warn't so. I tried it. Once I got a fishline, but no hooks. It warn't any good to me without hooks. I tried for the hooks three or four times, but somehow I couldn't make it work. By and by, one day, I asked Miss Watson to try for me, but she said I was a fool. She never told me why, and I couldn't make it out no way.
>
> I set down one time back in the woods, and had a long think about it. I says to myself, if a body can get anything they pray for, why don't Deacon Winn get back the money he lost on pork? Why can't the widow get back her silver snuffbox that was stole? Why can't Miss Watson fat up? No, says I to myself, there ain't nothing in it.[2]

And there "ain't," when we use it to present our demands to God. How much better is the centurion's example. He asks, but not for himself and not with presumption.

One Who Walks by Faith Feels Another's Pain

The officer's hurt is heard in his words: "Lord, my servant lies at home paralyzed and in terrible suffering" (Matthew 8:5). His servant's pain is his own. His empathy drives him to do whatever will ease the suffering.

Empathy is often overlooked as a source of spiritual strength. Cal Thomas understands its staying power.

When someone once referred to him as a Christian leader, the compliment bothered him. It betrayed a worldly value system. Musing on the meaning of the same Scripture that informs this book ("My power is made perfect in weakness"), Thomas sets the record straight.

> In a church I once attended, there was a man of tremendous faith. His wife is an alcoholic. His daughter has psychological problems. He was often poor in health. Yet, week after week, he never complained. He always smiled and asked me how I was doing. He faithfully brought to church a young blind man who had no transportation. He always sat with the blind man, helping him sing the hymns by saying the words into his ear. . . . That man was a "Christian leader" if ever there was one.[3]

I have experienced this empathy as the sufferer. To this day I carry vivid memories of the pain in my parents' eyes as they dealt with their feeble child during an attack of asthma. One incident in particular won't go away. I had walked to the county fairgrounds, just a couple of blocks away, to watch the carnival workers assemble the rides. For some reason, I was especially vulnerable that day to the dust and straw and assorted odors, so I quickly left. By the time I got home, I was nearly faint; breath would hardly come. My mother ran to the telephone to call Dad. She was scared and desperate. I had never seen her so frightened—nor so determined to get help no matter what she had to do. She felt my pain so acutely that nothing would prevent her from getting help for me.

Memories of Dad are different. Most of my troubles came at night, when I would wake up from sleep, panting and fighting for air. Dad was the lighter sleeper, so whenever I called out, he would come, lift me out of bed, and either hold me or set me on a chair to administer my medicine. When I recall how he never once expressed impatience, never seemed to resent losing his sleep on my account, I have trouble fighting tears. To me he was the epitome of patient strength.

Only years later, when our daughter Candy became so ill and it was my turn to play the parents' role, did I understand how much strength one is given in the taking care of a loved one. Joy and I often thanked God that He never gave us more than we could carry. More than that, Joy specifically thanked Him for the way He seemed to have prepared her for those difficult days.

Over the years, we had invited several young people to live with us for a time. A year before Candy's health crisis, we had taken in a young school teacher who lived that year with us — and who is still a member of our extended family. She was physically and emotionally exhausted when she moved in, and Joy tenderly nursed her back to health. Little did we suspect that Candy would require even more care, including her hospitalization and subsequent recuperation. At first, the doctors told us she was epileptic, but later we were able to associate her problems with severe food and other allergies. During the ordeal, Joy and I were both surprised at our ability to cope with her needs, care for the family, and still function on the job and in the rest of our other demand-filled lives.

I'm not sharing our experience because it is so unusual. To the contrary, its very ordinariness makes it applicable here. Few parents our age don't have their own story to tell of the time when through another's pain they discovered an inner strength they never suspected was there.

One more word I should add. As you can imagine, we had taken Candy from doctor to doctor, trying to solve her mysterious problem. We became pretty astute observers of medical practitioners along the way. Many times, after examining Candy, the doctors would conclude the real problem was not in her but in her neurotic mother. This report, often tearfully related, never failed to make me angry, since I had never known a less neurotic person than Joy. The doctors, afraid or unwilling to admit they were baffled by Candy's complex symptoms, assumed an air of superiority and strength—which rendered them weak and useless in her case.

Two doctors were our heroes. One, Dr. Jim Jay, admitted his ignorance and led us (he didn't simply direct but accompanied us) to the best specialist he knew (who unfortunately was one of the "superior" ones, so he did her no good). The other was Dr. Warren Miller, just beginning his practice, whose humility and sympathy enabled him to work with us until Candy was once again normal. Drs. Jay and Miller were, in our opinion, the real healers —because they hurt with us and, really caring, refused to pretend a strength they didn't have.

One Who Walks by Faith Doesn't Claim Any Rights

"Lord, I do not deserve to have you come under my roof" (Matthew 8:8). A Pharisee's petition might have sounded quite different: "God, I thank you that I am not like all other men—robbers, evildoers, adulterers—or even like this tax collector. I fast twice a week and give a tenth of all I get. *Therefore I am claiming your promise. I've done my part. Now grant me this healing. You owe it to me"* (Luke 18:11, 12, italicized portion is my addition).

The centurion's appeal has more in common with the tax collector of Jesus' parable: "Have mercy on me, a sinner" (Luke 18:13). He is conscious of his unworthiness, but he asks anyway. He may be weak, but he has found One with the strength he needs. He receives the blessing Jesus promises the "poor in spirit."

The whole encounter is a study in grace at work. Claiming no merit in himself, the centurion throws himself on the mercy of the strong One, who blesses him. Christ, demanding nothing of the supplicant, favors him with his servant's healing.

James Stewart tells of Dr. John Duncan, noted scholar, mystic, and theologian who knew the Hebrew language so well his students claimed he prayed to God at night in

Hebrew. One day, two of them, endowed with a healthy dose of skepticism, decided to spy on him at his prayers. They didn't hear Hebrew; instead they heard,

Gentle Jesus, meek and mild,
Look upon a little child
Pity my simplicity,
Suffer me to come to thee.[4]

The learned theologian comes to the Lord not on the strength of his academic achievements, but by the grace of God. He asks nothing but the right to come.

If Paul is right in claiming, "When I am weak, then I am strong," then we are wise to admit, "When I am strong, then I am weak." The strong want to do everything themselves, to "call the shots," to demand their rights, to do "their thing." So long as they do, they will not tap into the divine resources available to the weak.

An old joke that made its rounds a few years ago makes this as clear as anything can. A fellow was hiking on the mountain one day when a thick fog suddenly descended. In a matter of minutes, he could barely see and quickly lost his bearings. Even worse, he misstepped and fell. Fortunately, he was able to break his fall by grasping a protruding limb. He was down only a few feet from the trail, but too far to get back up. The cliff was a sheer drop; there were no hand holds.

The fog was so thick he couldn't see anything below; he had no idea how far it was to bottom.

In desperation he called, "Is there anybody up there?"

To his relief, a voice answered, "I am here."

"Who are you?"

"I am the Lord."

"Oh, Lord, can You help me?"

"Yes, I will help you."

"Oh, thank You, Lord. I'll do whatever You say."

Then the voice of the Lord spoke again: "Let go."

There was a pause, and then the fallen hiker called out again, "Is there anybody else up there?"

He was not yet ready for grace. He hadn't fully admitted the weakness of his position and wasn't ready to be poor in spirit or desperate enough to offer the trust of faith. He still had to call the shots, to choose from among options. So, at the story's end, he's still dangling there.

In every instance I shared above of our family's weaknesses, I have had to accept help. Only when I fully admitted my weakness could I draw on others' strength. Admitting was the hard part.

One Who Walks by Faith Needs No Spectacular Demonstration

"But just say the word, and my servant will be healed" (Matthew 8:8). The centurion had without a doubt been to other healers first. Don't you suppose he had had his fill of potions and prescriptions and incantations and all the mumbo jumbo the medical arts of his day offered? There was no shortage of quacks then, either. By this stage in his urgent search for healing, he wanted nothing more than the authoritative word, the quiet confidence of one who was in touch with divine power.

I don't know about you, but I am profoundly suspicious of the spectacular. Even Christian miracle workers leave me doubting. Physicians and preachers who promote their virtuosity turn me off. I listen much more gladly to someone like the late Swiss physician Paul Tournier. Once when he was speaking in Majorca, Spain, an American doctor stood up and asked, "Dr. Tournier, do you know any phony Christian therapists?"

"Ah, oui, C'est moi" ("It is I"), he answered, and waited for the next question.[5]

We can trust a doctor like him. He also wrote,

Christianity is not one ideology over against other ideologies. It is a life inspired by the Holy Spirit. Its victories are nothing but victories over itself, not over others. It propagates itself through humility and self-examination, not through triumphs.[6]

Humility doesn't demand spectacles. This was the problem Paul had to deal with in the Corinthian church. Christians there boasted they were possessed by the Spirit. They taunted others who didn't have their supernatural gifts. How strong they felt themselves — and how weak they really were. Boasting of their sanctification, they descended into sensualism.

To correct them, Paul called attention to the Crucified One. How dared they boast of their talents and abuse their freedom in the face of His death for them? What could they gain in showing off their so-called supernatural powers when their Savior only pointed to His weakness on a cross? Jesus boasted of nothing, except His devotion to His Father's will. Only in the Father's strength could He achieve anything. So He died, weakened unto death. His taunters were correct: He saved others but could not save himself.

He didn't have to.

One Who Walks by Faith Is More Unusual Than We Think

Now comes the hard part. Jesus addresses the crowd:

I say to you that many will come from the east and the west, and will take their places at the feast with Abraham, Isaac and Jacob in the kingdom of heaven. But the subjects of the kingdom will be thrown outside, into the darkness, where there will be weeping and gnashing of teeth (Matthew 8:11, 12).

Why will so many be excluded? Is it because they do not so much have faith in God as faith in their faith in God? Do they think too highly of themselves? Do they have more confidence in themselves than faith in Him? If so, then in their perceived strength they are weak indeed.

The centurion's faith, on the other hand, is characterized by obedience, submissiveness, and humility. The master becomes like those who serve him. They are his servants; he is Christ's.

The incident illustrates a serious American problem. Nearly every student of America is bewailing the decline of our once great nation. Symptomatic, they point out, is the failure of the public school system. Test scores are falling and, year by year, American school children increase in ignorance and decrease skills.

That's what objective studies show; but when you ask America's youth, you get a different opinion. In self-rating tests, seventy percent of American students tested rated themselves above average in leadership ability and only two percent below average. In ability to get along with others, *zero* percent of the 829,000 respondents rated themselves below average, sixty percent placed themselves in the top ten percent, and twenty-five percent saw themselves among the top one percent![7] They rate themselves strong! Yet they are weak. They need these words:

> When they measure themselves by themselves and compare themselves with themselves, they are not wise. . . . "Let him who boasts boast in the Lord." For it is not the one who commends himself who is approved, but the one whom the Lord commends (2 Corinthians 10:12, 17, 18).

All the classes in improving your self image and all the books on remaking yourself into the person you want to be are worthless if, in the end, you are one of those who "measure themselves by themselves and compare themselves with themselves."

We come to the end of the story. It's a happy ending. The centurion's servant is healed. The weak has been healed through a strength not his own.

This chapter is too long, yet I am aware of so many things I haven't said. For people who will admit their weakness, God provides many resources. Consider these:

Prayer. Who hasn't been strengthened by prayer — your own and others on your behalf?

Parents. Parents (at least the good ones) never quit caring, even when we would rather they wouldn't care quite so much.

Partners and friends. Is there any greater blessing than a steadfast friend, any greater strength than in knowing that special person is standing with you?

God himself, as experienced in the Holy Spirit, who abides and gives counsel and comfort.

All the healers who have served you: counselors, ministers, and physicians.

All the teachers, professional and lay, who have opened up a whole world of available assistance.

The Word of God, an endless source of inspiration and help in time of need.

When we walk by faith, we do not walk alone.

Notes

[1]Mark McCormack, *What They Don't Teach You at Harvard Business School* (New York: Bantam Books, Inc., 1984), pp. 68-71.

[2]Mark Twain, *The Adventures of Huckleberry Finn,* chapter 3.

[3]Cal Thomas, "What it Means to Be a Christian Leader," *Evangelical Newsletter,* June 8, 1984, p. 3.

[4]James S. Stewart, *The Wind of the Spirit* (Nashville: Abingdon Press, 1968), p. 133.

[5]Keith Miller, *The Scent of Love* (Waco: Word Books, 1983).

[6]"The Whole Person in a Broken World." Quoted in *Christianity Today,* December 13, 1985, p. 46.

[7]David G. Myers, *The Inflated Self.* Quoted in *The Seduction of Christianity* by Hunt and McMahon (Eugene: Harvest House, 1985), pp. 198, 199.

6

Everything I Need for Joy

Acts 8:26-39; Luke 19:1-10

After all these years, it's surprising how often I still think of him. I may even have written about him in one of my earlier books. (As we grow older we repeat our stories, I'm told. Perhaps. I can't remember.) I almost never read or hear of another handicapped person without Bill Bish's name coming to mind.

It happened when I was reading Max Lucado's *The Applause of Heaven*. He describes Robert Reed, who exclaimed, "I have everything I need for joy!" Lucado found it amazing that a man with twisted hands and useless feet, who couldn't bathe or feed himself, and whose speech betrayed the severity of his cerebral palsy, could pronounce himself joyful. The disease that kept him from walking couldn't keep him from graduating from Abilene Christian University with a degree in Latin. Neither could it bar him from teaching at a St. Louis junior college or becoming a missionary to Portugal.

He moved to Lisbon alone and rented a hotel room. He located a restaurant that would feed him after the rush hour and a tutor to instruct him in Portuguese. Stationing himself daily in a park, he distributed brochures about Christ. Six years later, he had seventy converts, one of whom he married.

This victim of one of our most highly dreaded diseases said he had everything he needed for joy.[1]

So did my friend Bill Bish, the victim of a formerly ter-
rifying disease: polio. Stricken as a boy, before he had
reached his full height, Bill's body twisted into a hunch-
back form, one nearly useless leg not much more than
bone wrapped in skin, his distorted torso crushed down
on his hip bones.

What happened to his body was not as cruel, however,
as the abuse he suffered at the hands of a thoughtless
society. Fortunately, Bill's parents loved him and so did
his church. While discouraging him from pursuing a
career in missions (which in those days usually meant
going into some primitive area), they encouraged his
walk with the Lord. In later life, Bill became one of the
strongest supporters of missions I have ever known. If he
couldn't go, he believed at least he could send.

I can't ever think of Bill without a smile. I have never
known a more generous, more considerate, more joyful
person. Nothing pleased him more than to arrange a gift
for someone, pay for it, and never let the recipient know
the source of the surprise. Never did I see him happier
than the evening he told me in his living room, fairly
bouncing in his chair as he did so, that that year he had
been able to give the Lord's work four tithes.

God had blessed him, this little man who began his
sales career pushing a baby buggy filled with Raleigh
products from house to house. By the time I knew him,
Bill was in his fifties and was one of Oregon's leading
State Farm Insurance salesmen. I knew him well, because
he and Elizabeth had bought a large house in the St.
Johns district of Portland so they could provide the
church secretary her own apartment upstairs and still
keep a room on the main floor for the part-time youth
directors who served the church in yearly or two-yearly
succession. I was one of the lucky ones to occupy it.

There's so much more I'd like to tell you about Bill and
Liz: how Bill's first wife Lucy's parents threatened to dis-
own her if she married that cripple; how they married

anyway, and reared three daughters; how Bill and Liz lost their first mates through illness; how she brought up her five children without a father in the midst of the depression; how Bill and Liz met and married in the church, the tall lady and the little man; how they took budding young ministers under their wings and taught them like a latter-day Priscilla and Aquila; how they spoiled their grandchildren; how they remembered the Lord's work even in their wills; and so much more.

But I must get on with this chapter. They came to mind, as I said, because of Robert Reed's profession of joy. Joy in spite of a rebellious body. (I'm having trouble leaving Bill behind. Have you noticed how joyful people are like magnets, drawing you toward themselves, brightening your day through their irrepressibility?)

And have you noticed how joyful people usually acquired their gladness "in spite of" and not "because of" their circumstances? The English writer J. M. Barrie believed that's because "joy has to be paid for." He said so in a letter to the Countess of Lyttelton, just after her husband died. He wrote, "If you had cared for him less, if he had been less worth caring for, the road would be less heavy-going. Joy has to be paid for."[2]

We must know this truth instinctively. Most of the stories we preachers relate to bring out the full meaning of the word have this "in spite of" quality, don't they? We are unimpressed with a story of a happy someone who is well born, well bred, well-fixed, and well-connected. We want to know more. We'll withhold judgment, thank you, until we hear the rest of the story. How will the apparently sanguine person react when, as we know it will, adversity finally hits? Will there still be a smile? Will he be able, in the words of James, to "count it all joy"?

That seems to be the difference between happiness and joy, doesn't it? Happiness has to do with good things "happening" to us. A new car makes us happy, or a raise, or a dozen-roses-surprise. Remember Charles Schulz's

Happiness Is a Warm Puppy? It is, when you are a child and the puppy is yours. But will the happiness survive through a serious accident in that car, or a lay-off, or a Dear John letter, or the puppy's death? If it does, we don't call it happiness anymore because something that doesn't depend on external circumstances has taken over. You have learned to say, with the apostle Paul,

> I have learned to be content whatever the circumstances. I know what it is to be in need, and I know what it is to have plenty. I have learned the secret of being content in any and every situation, whether well fed or hungry, whether living in plenty or in want" (Philippians 4:11, 12).

What he is talking about is an unwavering sense of well-being that will not be defeated by circumstance. If you can't understand this quality of joy, you will be baffled by Mother Teresa's answer to the *Time* interviewer who asked her, "What is the most joyful place that you have ever visited?"

> "Kalighat," she said. "When the people die in peace, in the love of God, it is a wonderful thing. To see our poor people happy together with their families, these are beautiful things. The joy of the poor people is so clean, so clear. The real poor know what is joy."

The contrast on *Time's* page,[3] by the way, says it all. On the right column is the conclusion of the interview, with a picture exactly in the center of Mother Teresa's worn old hands resting on her lap, the fingers of her right hand gently fondling her prayer beads. The other two columns contain a gaudy full-color advertisement for Las Vegas, the beautiful blonde woman dancer having leapt into the handsome young man's arms. Just below her leg is the caption: THE AMERICAN WAY TO PLAY. Then the text: "Sultry sexy nights. And lazy summer days. Wrapped around the most affordable excitement in the world. That's Las Vegas. Where luck gets its name."

There's your choice: joy or happiness, sacrificial ministry among the dying or superficial splendor among the playing. Put it to a vote, and America will, of course, elect Las Vegas. Sex, play, laziness, glitter, gold, good luck. These are the favored delights of the pursuers of happiness. So we vote for Las Vegas and turn our backs on the poor people of Calcutta. Yet deep within, we suspect the greater blessing is to be found in following the footsteps of the little servant lady to Calcutta. Hers is the way of giving, and Vegas's is the way of getting. Jesus had it right, "It is more blessed to give than to receive" (Acts 20:35). For "more blessed" read "more joyful."

One can't help wondering whether *Time*'s composing editor didn't have some spiritual insight as he so carefully juxtaposed those worn but loving hands beside the frivolously playful young Las Vegas players (whose uncalloused hands seem never to have touched dirt). Did the editor know the words of Thomas Aquinas, who mused, "No one can live without delight and that is why a man deprived of spiritual joy goes over to carnal pleasures"?[4]

It is easy to lose the distinction between joy and happiness (and thereby lose our way to life) because the two words are often used synonymously. For example, Dr. William Sheldon offers a definition of happiness that is actually an excellent understanding of joy: "Happiness is essentially a state of going somewhere, wholeheartedly, one-directionally, without regret or reservation."[5]

You can't listen to Mother Teresa more than a moment without realizing you are in the presence of someone who decided long ago where she wanted to go and how she wanted to get there — and she has gone there! She has no regrets. She gave herself without reservation. Hence the calm, the state of blessedness she communicates.

The people in the other column? They're having fun — that's obvious. But is it joy? Ask that after the dancing is over and the drinks have been drunk and the money has been gambled away and the wrinkles appear and the back can't lift the beautiful woman (who is no longer beautiful anyway) and she can't leap anymore.

When it's no longer fun, will you still go "wholeheartedly, one-directionally, without regret or reservation"? Then it wasn't mere happiness; it was joy. It's the difference between the young people's dance (which goes around and around but doesn't go anywhere) and the journey.

To be fair, I must admit there's place for both the dance and the journey in life. Celebration is an essential expression of life's blessings. Some things do make us happy, and we show it. Nothing in this chapter should be taken as a complaint against laughter and singing and occasional frivolity. My purpose is simply to say a word in favor of the joy that sustains us when the laughter is silent.

Vernon Grounds defines this joy as

> the deep down exuberance which comes from God through His Spirit by faith in His Son, regardless of outward circumstances or interpersonal relationships. Joy is supernatural in its source and essence, a foretaste of the face-to-face communion with God that will be rapture forever.[6]

That's a mouthful, but a tasty one. "Deep down exuberance." It's a welling up from the depths, a bubbling up of the overflow, a sense that "it is well with my soul," and that wellness doesn't depend on the props that Las Vegas happiness must have or it collapses. Yes, it's supernatural; it comes from above and leads us in that direction.

Joy is Jesus' goal for us. "I have told you this so that my joy may be in you and that your joy may be complete" (John 15:11). We like the sound of these words, don't we? You'd think we'd speak more about them in Christian circles than we do. We may hesitate because of the "this" in His sentence: "I have told you this." We need to read the preceding two verses in John 15 to grasp His intent:

"As the Father has loved me, so have I loved you. Now remain in my love. If you obey my commands, you will remain in my love, just as I have obeyed my Father's commands and remain in his love."

There's the rub: first comes the obedience, then the joy that springs out of loving and being loved by the Lord.

Things are turning serious, aren't they? When we talk about obedience in relation to joy, our Las Vegas couple bow out. They have nothing to say. We can learn more from the saintly little lady. She doesn't use C. S. Lewis's words, but her life expresses it: "Joy is the serious business of Heaven."[7]

In Acts 8:26-39, an angel dispatches Philip to tend to this Heavenly business. He is to find an Ethiopian official (either a convert to Judaism or a "God-fearer," a person seeking to learn more of the God of Israel) poring over Isaiah 53. Christians would later refer to this section as messianic; that is, a prophecy describing the coming Christ. The Ethiopian doesn't understand it that way. In fact, he doesn't understand it at all.

His confusion is Philip's opportunity, so beginning with this very passage Philip explains "the good news about Jesus" to the official.

The dialogue, as Luke has summarized it, doesn't mention baptism, but Philip must have included its significance in his explanation because the Ethiopian exclaims, "Look, here is water. Why shouldn't I be baptized?"

And he is. And he goes on his way "rejoicing." Philip's transaction with the man is complete, and as is inevitable when Heaven's business is transacted, the result is *joy*.

It was through his own conversion C. S. Lewis learned that Heaven's serious business is joy. In his autobiography, appropriately named *Surprised by Joy*, Lewis recounts his going to Whipsnade Zoo with his brother Warren for a picnic. Both men recorded the event in their diaries. Warren noted they were especially attracted by a "delightful brown plethoric [bear] which sat up and saluted for buns.

Jack [C. S.] is full of the dream of adding a pet bear to our private menagerie, which he intends to christen 'Bultitude.'" (The "Mr. Bultitude" of Lewis' book *That Hideous Strength* was undoubtedly drawn from this experience.)

But something far more important (though less obvious to his brother) was happening to Lewis. He writes,

> When we set out I did not believe that Jesus Christ is the Son of God, and when we reached the zoo I did. Yet I had not exactly spent the journey in thought. Nor in great emotion. "Emotional" is perhaps the last word we can apply to some of the most important events. It was more like when a man, after a long sleep, still lying motionless in bed, becomes aware that he is now awake.[8]

More awake, we might add, than ever before, more fully aware of God and life and oneself, even the less savory aspects of oneself, as in the case of the New Testament's Zacchaeus.

In Luke 19, Jesus meets Zacchaeus, who has long been one of my favorites. I first identified with him in Sunday school, when we sang,

> Zacchaeus was a wee little man,
> a wee little man was he.
> He climbed up in the sycamore tree,
> for the Lord he wanted to see.

When the Lord spots him in his perch, He invites himself to the tax collector's home for dinner. The Bible reports that Zacchaeus "came down at once and welcomed him *gladly*" (Luke 19:6).

The proof of the *gladness* (a synonym for *joy* here) is evident in what follows. Luke zeroes in on Zacchaeus's dramatic change of heart. The publican, who seems to have on his conscience more than one questionable tax transaction, cannot continue conducting his affairs as usual.

Jesus has captivated him. He can't associate with the Master and be unethical at the office.

"Look, Lord! Here and now I give half of my possessions to the poor, and if I have cheated anybody out of anything, I will pay back four times the amount" (Luke 19:8).

Here's physical proof a spiritual conversion has occurred. Jesus assures him that "today salvation has come to this house . . . " (Luke 19:9). Zacchaeus, snubbed by Jewish society because of his profession, is a true "son of Abraham," according to Jesus, who believes a person's descent from Abraham is proved by his active faith rather than by his genealogy. (Paul reflects this thought; see Romans 4:12.) Zacchaeus's conversion is genuine, it is apparent, because it has reached every level of his character. The loner now wants reconciliation with those he has cheated; the lover of money has discovered a higher love. He who received Jesus gladly has entered into joy.

Before adopting the New International Version of the Bible for personal and pulpit use, I regularly relied on the Revised Standard Version. In most ways, I prefer the NIV, but I do miss the RSV's translation of Acts 2:46. It's a good text to use with Zacchaeus's conversion story: "And day by day, attending the temple together and breaking bread in their homes, they [the first Christians] partook of food with *glad* and *generous* hearts. . . . "

There you have it: glad and generous. When Zacchaeus received Jesus gladly (joyfully), generosity naturally followed. It isn't possible, is it, to feel gladness and be stingy? Generosity is the mark of joy.

These were the marks of Old Testament festivals, which were even called "your times of rejoicing" (Numbers 10:10). These feasts were the appointed times for bringing to the Lord offerings, accompanied by singing and laughing and dancing. The Israelites were ordered to "sacrifice fellowship offerings there, eating them and rejoicing in the presence of the Lord your God" (Deuteronomy 27:7).

In Luke's history of the young church, he reports the apostles, having been unjustly arrested, tried, flogged, and forbidden to speak the name of Jesus, "left the Sanhedrin, rejoicing because they had been counted worthy of suffering disgrace for the name" (Acts 5:41). Theirs was a sacrifice of a different kind, but they who were so generously giving everything they had for the Lord were experiencing a joy transcending their punishment.

The Bible says that "God loves a cheerful giver" (1 Corinthians 9:7). Can there be any other kind of genuine giving? The spirit of generosity and the spirit of joy are simply inseparable. Put another way: "The bird of paradise alights only upon the hand that does not grasp."[9]

Remember those careworn, giving hands in *Time*'s picture? They are the symbol of joy.

Notes

[1]Max Lucado, *The Applause of Heaven* (Waco: Word Publishing, 1990), pp. 6, 7.

[2]William Barclay quotes Barrie in his *Testament of Faith* (London and Oxford: Mowbrays, 1975), p. 54.

[3]*Time*, December 4, 1989, p. 14.

[4]Quoted in *The Wisdom of the Saints*, ed. Jill Haak Adels (New York, Oxford: Oxford Press, 1987), p. 191.

[5]Harry Emerson Fosdick quotes Dr. Sheldon in *On Being a Real Person* (New York and London: Harper and Brothers, 1943), p. 32.

[6]I read this in Gary Collins' *The Joy of Caring* (Waco: Word Books, 1980), p. 18. He read it in J. Allen Thompson's "Gather the Harvest With Joy," in *Harvest Today*, 33:3-5.

[7]Walter Hooper, ed., *The Business of Heaven, Readings from C. S. Lewis* (Great Britain: Collins Fount Paperbacks, 1984), p. 19.

[8]Roger Lancelyn Green and Walter Hooper, *C. S. Lewis: A Biography* (New York: Harcourt, Brace and Jovanovich, 1974), p. 116.

[9]Quoted in *Forbes*, November 26, 1990, p. 320.

7

SOMETHING THAT BATTERS — OR BETTERS — YOUR SOUL

Matthew 13:1-9, 18-23

When I was a senior in high school, Norman Anderson, our unforgettable English teacher, assigned an essay to be written on the subject, "The pen is mightier than the sword." Never before had I given much thought to the power of words. Until then, had you asked me to compare the effectiveness in world affairs of arms and speeches or essays, I'd have laughed. I was born just before World War II and entered high school during the Korean conflict. Of course, I knew that bombs and bullets were more persuasive than all the words of all the politicians on earth.

Then I sat down to write my essay. Only then, and only slowly, did I become conscious that behind every armed conflict were leaders shouting words at one another. The guns did the damage, but the words aimed the guns. Later, when I read John F. Kennedy's praise of Churchill for mobilizing the English language and sending *it* into battle, I understood what he was talking about.

When Anatoli Scharansky was released to return to Israel after nine years in Soviet prisons and work camps, stripped of most of his other possessions, he said he had clung to the miniature copy of the *Book of Psalms* his wife had sent from Israel. It was so valuable to him he once paid 130 days in solitary confinement for refusing to yield it to the authorities. As he was about to be released, his guards tried once more to seize it. Again he refused.

"I said I would not leave without the Psalms that had helped me so much. . . . I lay down in the snow and said, 'Not another step.'"

They examined the book carefully, then gave it back to him.[1]

The guards were helpless to control a man controlled by the Psalmists' words. Words strengthen us in our weakness. But not just any words will do. They must be the right words, and they must be spoken to ready listeners.

Jesus bases His parable of the sower (Matthew 13:1-9, 18-23) on this truth. When the right words ("the message about the kingdom") are received by a ready listener ("the man who hears the word and understands it"), the result is a terrific crop ("a hundred, sixty or thirty times what was sown").

It matters what we hear and how we hear it.

What We Hear

My son Lane and I were talking about the impact people have on us. We agreed we both have to be very careful in selecting our friends, since they affect our moods and attitudes more strongly than we like to admit. Not only are we influenced by people, but by what we read, what movies we see, and what we watch on television— especially what we watch on television. Since most Americans have their sets on six or seven hours a day, TV is the single most influential mind and mood controller in America. It constantly feeds us information. And, regrettably, we do become like what we feed our minds.

Of course, how much we take in depends on how ready we are to receive. In Jesus' parable, there are three other kinds of soil besides the ready, receptive kind.

Some soil is hard, like the path through a field. The good words can't penetrate at all. Jesus equates this soil with people who can't understand what they are hearing.

Some is shallow, like the thin layer of dirt over rocky places. Persons like this, Jesus says, are superficial. In them the good words can't take root. At first they like what they hear, receiving it gladly, but then, for whatever reasons, they soon accommodate something else in its place. They don't discriminate among the kinds of words they hear.

Finally, there is the thorn-infested soil. Jesus uses this language to describe "the man who hears the word, but the worries of this life and the deceitfulness of wealth choke it, making it unfruitful" (Matthew 13:22).

One of Walker Percy's characters in *The Second Coming* asks, "If the good news is true, why is no one pleased to hear it?" His question is a good introduction to Jesus' parable.

(A parable, explains P. G. Wodehouse, "is one of those stories in the Bible which sounds at first like a pleasant yarn, but keeps something up its sleeve which suddenly pops up and knocks you flat."[2])

They aren't pleased to hear it because, since they have fed so long on a different diet, or have heard it from unattractive spokesmen,[3] these the words of the kingdom don't sound like good news at first — or second — thought.

It's Powerful

Yet, if Jesus is right, there is productive power in these words. The French skeptic Voltaire predicted, "Within 100 years of my death, the Bible will be extinct." He died in 1778. No one reads Voltaire anymore, except a few college students of philosophy and the humanities. The Bible, on the other hand, endures on the best seller lists, and millions of readers testify to its life-changing impact.

Let me tell you just one story to illustrate the superior power of pen to sword. (Have you ever wondered why the Bible speaks of the Word of God as the "sword of the Spirit"? If it's arms you want, you can't find anything more powerful than the Spirit armed with God's Word.)

The story is about Gregory the Great, the Benedictine monk who became Pope of the Church of Rome. His goal was to extend the domain of the church over the entire world. A specific target was up to the far north, Britain and Gaul (roughly modern France). He knew this wouldn't be an easy conquest. Julius Caesar had tried before, but his six legions couldn't plant a permanent Roman colony there. In place of Caesar's six legions, Gregory sent forty Benedictine monks. In lieu of the legion's full armor, Gregory outfitted his monks with love and the Bible and some hymns he had composed. Instead of coming to take the natives' land away from them, the monks took nothing away but added faith and a new culture to the land. They presented their special Book with its special words to their Anglo-Saxon hosts, and, to help them even more, they brought along grammar books and primers with which to found schools to teach our English ancestors to read the good words.[4] Where Julius Caesar's legions failed, Gregory's monks triumphed.

The amazing collapse of communism in the late twentieth century is further proof of the power of good words. Many years ago, during one of my first visits to an iron curtain country, I became convinced communism couldn't last long. Any government based on an ideology so alien to people's hearts that its citizens could be kept inside the country's borders only at gunpoint is doomed. Such an ideology cannot forever withstand the force of the benevolent Word from God.

It's Revealing

Perhaps the unreceptive soil Jesus talks about may have shut out the good words because they are too revealing—not just revealing about God, but exposing the hearer as well. Every Christian can testify that we don't just read the Bible; it reads us and reads us precisely.

Christian poet Li-Young Lee, whose poems have been shaped by his reading of the Bible, asks, "Can you know a person by reading his Bible?" Lee had not been close to his father, who had once been personal physician to Communist Chairman Mao before he fell from favor. He had also been a vice-president of an Indonesian medical college, a philosopher and linguist, a political prisoner in a leper colony, and, after his escape, a Presbyterian minister in a small Pennsylvania village. Lee knew these facts about his father, but didn't know the real man—until he inherited his father's library. "When I opened his Bible and read the marginalia," Lee says, "there was a part of him that opened up to me."[5] A part hidden before. His father's written response to the good words on the pages let his son see aspects of him he had not known before.

I don't write on the margins. Perhaps it's in fear someone will read my scribblings. But like Lee's father, I cannot read the Bible without introspection. Parts of it read like a personal letter from God to me, requiring response, demanding repentance, encouraging another try, offering hope. Other sections scold or challenge or demand change. No other book so forcefully reveals me as I am. Perhaps that's why, when I'm feeling especially rebellious or grouchy, I can't bear to read it at all. I don't want to know any more about me. I don't care to be changed.

Certain Scriptures force you to get up and get on with your walk with God. They charge you to. . . .
Take up your cross and follow. . . .
Bear one another's burdens. . . .
Love one another. . . .
Go . . . and make disciples. . . .
Forgive men their sins. . . .
Love your enemies. . . .
Seek first his kingdom and his righteousness. . . .
Ask and it will be given to you. . . .
Repent and be baptized. . . .
Take my yoke upon you. . . .
Have no other gods before me. . . .
Choose this day whom you will serve. . . .

What I am saying is this: these good words impact all relationships in which they are taken seriously. When we follow Christ, taking up our cross, bearing one another's burdens in love, making disciples, forgiving and loving our enemies, seeking first His righteousness, and all the rest that goes with putting Christ first in our lives, we change, our relationships change, and, having seen ourselves in the light of God's word, we permit His Spirit to transform us for the better. Our priorities are straightened out, and our relationships are improved. They're "a hundred, sixty or thirty times" better!

Joanie Grimm once gave the perfect example of how this all works when she told of the day she overheard her husband, David, talking to a young man who thought he'd like to marry their daughter. David felt he had to warn the suitor about her. "She's like her mother," he said. "You'll never be first in her life. Christ is."

"How does that work?" the young man asked.

"It's okay," he was reassured, "because she's not first in my life either."

Joanie was proud of her husband's explanation and proud of the relationship they enjoy because neither one is first. They have taken Christ's words seriously. Because they have, He rules; they don't.

It's Motivating

We can't talk about the revealing nature of God's Word without noting how motivational it is. Revealing the real you, the good words make you want to be better, to do better.

You can't stand the status quo in your spiritual life. You can't, that is, if you are "good soil." Among the perplexities in ministry are those church attenders who have sat and politely listened to my sermons for well over a decade now, with no discernible response. They heroically resist the good words. I can't understand them. Certainly I can accept their rejection of *my* words, since they carry no authority and little credibility, but my sermons are always based on *His* good words.

I'm not alone in my frustration. Richard Halverson, our popular U. S. Senate chaplain, was grumbling about the same thing clear back in the mid-fifties, when he was a local church pastor.

> Here then, is another reason for lukewarm, fed-up Christianity: Those Church members who simply refuse to go along with Jesus Christ beyond the point of comfortable convention and propriety. They will patronize Him, admire Him, tip the hat to Him, give Him an hour in church on Sunday morning, but they will not serve Him. If commitment is involved, they fall back—unwilling to pay the price of true discipleship. Obviously such people will become disinterested and indifferent. If Jesus Christ is not taken seriously, He will sooner or later be left alone![6]

What is so tragic is not only that they just sit there, but that by not taking the good words into their hearts and yielding to their motivating power, they deprive themselves of the abundant life Jesus has promised. They remain what they seem: respectable, comfortable, ordinary, non-productive and rather dull.

Is the fault, I have often wondered, all in the soil and not in the sower? In the parable, there's nothing wrong with the farmer's technique. Jesus' whole focus is on the receptivity of the hearers. In my case, however, I am more critical of the sower. Have I prepared well enough; have I presented honestly enough; have I been too timid? My style is certainly not like the famous seventeenth-century poet and preacher John Donne, who has written,

> It is not God's ordinary way to be whispering of secrets. For Publication of Himself He hath constituted a Church. And in this Church, His Ordinance is Ordinance indeed; His Ordinance of preaching *batters the soul*, and by that breach,

the Spirit enters; His Ministers are an *Earthquake*, and *shake an earthly soul*; they are the *sounds of thunder*, and *scatter* a cloudy conscience.[7]

Jesus' good words are patently not trinkets to be toyed with; there is an element of violence in good preaching, and Donne is a master of it. I, on the other hand, wishing to be diplomatic and inoffensive, may be shielding those whose defenses need shattering. Whatever the fault, something isn't happening that should, because whenever these good words of the gospel meet a heart ready to hear, things happen. The gospel is motivational.

It's Sustaining

What we need most, of course, is not motivation to perform some extraordinary deed for Jesus. The greater challenge is simply to remain faithful to Him in the deadly everydayness of life. We are not often tempted to commit gross sins; ours are rather the little cheatings, the unseen unfaithfulnesses, the silent denials of the faith. We require constant input of the good words to hold us true to our best selves.

Jesus was sustained in the wilderness in just this way. We often think of His temptation, recorded in Matthew 4, as a great contest between the evil one and the Good One. That may be what it was. I'm not so certain. Having been in the Judean wilderness, I picture this more as the quiet, mental debate that would inevitably occur in almost any mind. It was hot out there, and lonely, and food was scarce. His mind couldn't help wandering, could it? Who was there to hold it on the subject? And what was the subject? What conversation was possible?

Why shouldn't He think about fame or power or doing little tricks to make food for himself?

He was, after all, in human flesh.

What kept Him sane? Some good words, learned long before, came to His rescue when He needed them.

Man does not live on bread alone, but on every word that comes from the mouth of God. . . .

Do not put the Lord your God to the test. . . .

Worship the Lord your God, and serve him only (Matthew 4:4, 7, 10).

They sustained Him through the dry places. The good words are designed to do this, as the Psalmist knew:

I have hidden your word in my heart
   that I might not sin against you (Psalm 119:11).
Your word is a lamp to my feet
   and a light for my path (Psalm 119:105).

The good words sustained some American prisoners in Vietnam. To maintain their sanity, several men in a prison camp decided to put together a Bible from memory. Every participant contributed the verses he could recall. The exercise bolstered their personal faith (fed on the good words) and strengthened them in their bitterest trials.

God's Word does the same for us.

It's Liberating

This is maybe its most important quality—at least to me. Jesus promised, "If you hold to my teaching, you are really my disciples. Then you will know the truth, and the truth will set you free" (John 8:31, 32).

Free from what? That what's so wonderful about this promise. Free from so many things:

Free from false religions and phony philosophies.

Free from controllers and manipulators.

Free from the subtle lures of the prevailing culture.

Free from immature dependency on, or rebellions against, parents and other authority figures.

Free even from one's religious teachers.

The last item is especially important to me as a pastor. Another of my concerns is dependent church members.

They are sermon tasters, content to warm their pews and share their views of the current pastor's strengths and weaknesses, but they don't move on to maturity. They are unable to stand on their own spiritual feet.

My longtime friend Herb Works, who has spent the last several years preparing men and women for overseas missions service, gave me a copy of a brochure his agency, the Christian Missionary Fellowship, was giving to prospective candidates: *How Do You Know a CMF Prospect When You See One?* was its title. It listed several of the requisite qualities: faithfulness, flexibility, sense of humor, willingness to submit to authority, perseverance, correct concept of self-esteem. My eyes stopped, though, when I came to this one:

> Ability to Feed Oneself Spiritually. A person who is dependent on extra-ordinary weekly preaching and outstanding Bible study groups, in order to grow spiritually, will starve overseas.

"Amen!" I said aloud. Such a person will indeed starve overseas — and be overstuffed at home. He's always taking in, never giving out; always depending, never being depended on; keen to hear the familiar, critical of any challenging new thought.

I haven't been alone in my concern. William Temple came to the same conclusion after years of service in the Anglican Church.

> The church in latter years has relearned how to worship, but not in anything like the same degree how to understand. The congregation expects to gather for worship, it does not expect also to learn.[8]

But learn it must, or it condemns the preacher to repeating platitudes, judging him acceptable by the unoriginality of his thinking. Members hear what they've heard; they accept what they already know. But nothing new is allowed to take root, so there is no fruit.

I've said enough about what we need to hear. I hope I have convinced you the Bible can indeed transform a person's life. But whether it does depends on one thing.

How You Hear It

There is only one test of good hearing: a fruitful crop.

One can't help wondering what Jesus would have thought of English actor Alex McCowen's 1978 theatrical performance of the Gospel of Mark. It was what they call in the theater a *tour de force*, "a feat of remarkable skill." Dressed casually, he strolled on stage, opened his mouth, and recited the entire gospel from memory. *Time* magazine applauded, calling it "compelling theater that is at the same time nontheatrical." The telling comment, though, was reserved for the final paragraph: "As delivered by McCowen, *Mark* is a triumph of the human voice and the English language."[9]

McCowen's one-man show was a hit. People flocked to theaters to hear the Word spoken. It was good theater.

The words would undoubtedly burn in their hearts. Until the next play. They wouldn't abide. They hadn't taken root. They weren't supposed to. They were spoken in a theater, to hearers of the word only.

But the good words of the Sower were never intended to rival Shakespeare. They weren't designed to be poetry, pleasing to the ear, captivating to a theater audience. No, they are words to live by, to grow by. To produce fruit by.

The paradox of God's good words is this: they make us stronger or weaker, depending on what we do with them. When we hear the words and do them, like Jesus' wise man (Matthew 7:24-27), they make us strong enough to withstand storms. When we hear and do nothing, we make ourselves weaker than we would have been without them. We only fool ourselves if we think that by hearing or reading His words we have done something

God-pleasing and have a right to expect some protection from Him in exchange for our piety. Such is the religion of pagans.

Of such is not the kingdom of Heaven.

Who then is the good soil? "By their fruit you will recognize them" (Matthew 7:20).

They are the strong ones.

Notes

[1]*Time*, February 14, 1986, p. 36.

[2]Quoted in William J. Richardson, *The Restoring Father* (Cincinnati: Standard Publishing Company, 1987), p. 11.

[3]Walker Percy's character in *The Second Coming* is pretty hard on what Christians do to the good news. The earlier quotation follows this musing: "I am surrounded by Christians. They are generally speaking a pleasant and agreeable lot, not noticeably different from other people—even though they, the Christians of the South, the U. S. A., the Western world, have killed off more people than all other people put together. Yet I cannot be sure they don't have the truth. But if they have the truth, why is it the case that they are repellent precisely to the degree that they embrace and advertise the truth? One might even become a Christian if there were few if any Christians around." Quoted in Phillip Yancey, *I Was Just Wondering* (Grand Rapids: Wm. B. Eerdmans Publishing Company, 1989), p. 102.

[4]Rene Fulop-Miller, *The Saints That Rule the World* (Thomas Y. Crowell Company, 1945), p. 80.

[5]David Neff, "Remembering the Man Who Forgot Nothing," *Christianity Today*, September 2, 1988, p. 63.

[6]*Christian Maturity* (Los Angeles: Cowman Pulications, 1956), p. 29.

[7]Quoted in James S. Stewart, *Heralds of God* (London: Hodder and Stoughton, Ltd., 1946), pp. 210, 211. Italics mine.

[8]*Daily Readings From William Temple* (London: Hodder and Stoughton, St. Paul House), p. 137.

[9]*Time*, September 18, 1978, p. 100.

8

STRONGER
THAN VOODOO

Luke 18:9-14; Romans 8:26, 27

If any part of our spirituality feels weak, it's our prayer life. Prayer is almost as natural as breathing, yet most of us feel inhibited, undisciplined, and ineffective. Like the disciples, we cry, "Lord, teach us to pray," but, before the lesson is done, our minds drift to something else.

It's even worse when, because you are a pastor and are supposed to be good at these things, you try to say something helpful about prayer and you know you have no right to teach others what you yourself have not mastered.

In spite of my inadequacy on the subject, however, I must address it in a book about "a strength not my own." What Christian has ever confessed no need for prayer, no experience of power granted through prayer? Who would not agree with Dr. Alexis Carrel?

Prayer is the *most powerful form of energy* that one can generate. The influence of prayer on the human mind and body is as demonstrable as that of secreting glands. Its result can be measured in terms of increased physical buoyancy, greater intellectual vigor, moral stamina and a deeper understanding of the realities underlying human relationships. True prayer is a way of life.[1]

Even a child can experience this power, as the four-year-old Robert Louis Stevenson found out. He told his mother you can't be good without trying. He knew it, he said, because he had tried.

A mature adult also experiences it. Abraham Lincoln said of himself in this often repeated quotation, "I have been driven many times to my knees by the overwhelming conviction that I had nowhere else to go. My own wisdom and that of all about me seemed insufficient for that day."

Young and old alike testify to the efficacy of prayer. So will I, though I claim no expertise as I write. Two Scriptural passages give me comfort. Because of them, I can dare this chapter.

The first is another of Jesus' stories. This simple parable gives someone like me the courage to approach the Father. I quickly recognize myself. You might think, because I'm a clergyman, I would identify with the Pharisee's strong points (and perhaps even his failures), but I'm much more comfortable in the presence of the tax collector.

Two men went up to the temple to pray, one a Pharisee and the other a tax collector. The Pharisee stood and prayed about himself: "God, I thank you that I am not like other men—robbers, evildoers, adulterers—or even like this tax collector. I fast twice a week and give a tenth of all I get" (Luke 18:10-12).

Parts of this religious leader's litany of self-praise come uncomfortably close to home. I don't rob, I'm not an adulterer, I don't deliberately do evil. And I confess I am grateful not to be like some people I know. But I can't take the pride in what I am not, or even in what I do (like the tithing and fasting), because beneath all my showy religiosity there lurks a heart much more like the tax collector's: "God, have mercy on me, a sinner" (Luke 18:13).

My praying is often difficult because, when I am trying to hold my slippery consciousness on God, my conscience

94

shouts for attention, cruelly bringing up this recent sin or that recurring habit. My pulpit eloquence is silenced. Tears and regret tell Him what my tongue is too cowardly to confess. I know who I am, and I know He knows, too. I have nothing to offer but nothingness, nothing to hope in but His grace.

I told you there are two Scriptures. The second one is Romans 8:26, 27. To it we can cling when we are weak; it gives us strength.

> In the same way, the Spirit helps us in our weakness. We do not know what we ought to pray for, but the Spirit himself intercedes for us with groans that words cannot express. And he who searches our hearts knows the mind of the Spirit, because the Spirit intercedes for the saints in accordance with God's will.

When We Don't Know What or How to Pray

In truth, we know more than we give ourselves credit for. We may not have satisfied our yearning for a richer prayer life, but, even at our worst, we aren't hopeless. There are some things we just won't do, for example. We have outgrown the Christmas-list kind of prayer, and we aren't content with "God bless everybody" generalizations, and we don't treat prayer like some kind of black magic.

It was only when I ran across an article on voodooism, that I ever thought to give myself and Christians in general any credit for some things we *don't* do in prayer. It's easy to forget just how manipulative or even cruel some kinds of prayers can be. Voodoo, for example, exploits prayer and magic to control hapless victims. This formula for a love charm shows how it works:

> Take powdered angleworm dust mixed with love powder and ground John the Conqueror root. Place the above articles

in a small bag with a string on each end of the bag so as to meet around the waist. This charm will make your lover or sweetheart come to you and stay.

That's harmless enough, I suppose, unless you are the reluctant lover. But what if you wanted to break up a couple? This is a little less innocent:

Write the name of one party eight times and the name of the other party once across the name of the other on a piece of paper. Take the heart out of a red onion and put in the paper, together with red pepper and salt. Put the heart back into the onion and bury it upside down with the onion showing slightly above the ground.

It still is not too potent, but it does cater to a meddling mind. Should you wish to sicken or punish an enemy, however, here's all you have to do:

Take a soiled undergarment of theirs, hang on a bare rafter, and get some hackberry switches and whip the garment. They will be so sore they won't be able to get out of bed.[2]

What are these but prayers gone to war, calls upon spiritual forces to do your bidding? They are symbolic invocations of the gods or spirits to make your wishes come true.

There's a world of difference between the content and aim of the Christian's prayers and those of the voodoo practitioner. Christians can't ask for their God's help in hurting their enemies. To the contrary, "I tell you: Love your enemies and pray *for* [not *against*] those who persecute you" (Matthew 5:44, italics mine). Further, in the New Testament, disciples of Christ are never encouraged to pray for God's particularistic intervention (such as asking God to reveal His specific will for us in such things as which career to pursue, what house to buy, or, for that matter, even whom to marry or when). As Tom Sine points out, nowhere does Jesus pray "for guidance as to where to stay in the next town" or "about career decisions for one of his followers." For that matter, even though we have many of Paul's recorded prayers, we never read, "Father, show me whether I should get a job tentmaking for a while," or, "Show Timothy whether or not he should get married." Sine adds that, with all the advice Paul offers on singleness and marriage, he never instructs people on how to find "the will of God on whom and when to marry."[3]

When Jesus' disciples ask to be taught to pray, Jesus does include God's will, but in a very general way:

Your kingdom come,
your will be done
on earth as it is in heaven (Matthew 6:10).

That simple petition, along with asking for daily bread, for forgiveness, and for deliverance from the evil one, was enough.

On the other hand, in Luke's Gospel Jesus does tell a couple of stories to encourage us to pray with persistence for some very particular things (Luke 11:1-13; 18:1-8). In those cases, however, his subject was perseverance, and neither story had to do with asking God's help in making a decision.

What have we said so far? That prayer must be more than an attempt to manipulate spiritual forces to satisfy some whim of ours (as in black magic or voodoo or spiritualism) and that certain particularistic requests have no New Testament precedent. But what, then, are we to pray for, and how are we to do it?

In the Romans 8 passage, the New International Version literally translates the Greek as "what we ought to pray for," although the marginal note leaves room for the possibility of "how we ought to pray." Whether "what" or "how" matters little to us, since we don't do either well. We have trouble praying because. . . .

— we can't see the future, so sometimes we ask amiss.

— our feelings get in the way, blinding and distorting our perspective.

— we are ignorant of God's will.

So we don't know what's best for us or best for others for whom we are praying or even always best for God's work on earth. We know so little and feel so unworthy.

So why pray at all? Why try, when we aren't up to it, when we don't even know what to ask for?

If you think I'm exaggerating, let me quote from one more qualified than I, the eminent German theologian Helmut Thielicke. He warns us, before we start asking God for anything, to be pretty certain what we need. But that is exactly the problem. How do we know?

> To be able to present serious, worthy petitions I would really have to know what I need. . . . I would have to be capable of correctly interpreting my own life, other people's, indeed the life of the world itself. But can I do this? So, e.g., I pray I may get well, but in reality my most bitter need is to remain longer in the school of suffering. I pray I may have a successful career or win the sweepstakes, whereas God needs me in some altogether different place, and knows that success and money would be poison to my character. In the midst of a war I pray for the gift of peace; but God knows that we must drink the cup to its dregs. Thus in my prayers I make all kinds of false diagnoses, false estimates, & false interpretations of the real situation. And therefore our prayers are often merely foolish talk.

You see? I'm not exaggerating. Should we just not pray then? No, because God is not offended when our prayers seem a little improper.

But have we fathers and mothers ever taken it amiss when our children talked nonsense to us, when they asked us to buy them a horse or a Cadillac or a jet plane? . . . So in our prayers we ask, then add, "Thy will be done."[4]

Thielicke writes in the spirit of Romans 8:26. Of course, we make mistakes in our asking. Yes, our motives sometimes lead us astray and our petitions are terribly untactful and our words betray our ignorance of God's will and even of what's best for us. But we may ask anyway, because He invites us to. And because He helps us in our asking. We can bring to him what words can utter and, in our extremity, what J. B. Phillips calls somewhere "those agonizing longings which never find words."

James Montgomery's description is pretty accurate:

Prayer is the soul's sincere desire,
Unuttered or expressed,
The motion of a hidden fire
That trembles in the breast.
Prayer is the burden of a sigh,
The falling of a tear,
The upward glancing of an eye
When none but God is near.

And, amazingly, God invites the glance.
The Spirit helps us.
Prayer is not a solitary effort. We pray in partnership, our timid thoughts bolstered by the Holy Spirit.

For you did not receive a spirit that makes you a slave again to fear, but you received the Spirit of sonship. And by him we cry, "*Abba*, Father." The Spirit himself testifies with our spirit that we are God's children (Romans 8:15, 16).

And pray in the Spirit on all occasions with all kinds of prayers and requests. With this in mind, be alert and always keep on praying *for all the saints* (Ephesians 6:18, italics mine).

In these verses, praying "in the Spirit" does not refer to glossolalia, speaking in tongues. All Christians, not just speakers in tongues, can pray with the assurance that the Spirit "intercedes for us."

Nels Ferre has written of "Mother Alice" Kahokuoluna of the Kalaupapa Leper Colony in Hawaii. Speaking humbly in chapel to her fellow seminarians, she confessed, "I have come to the seminary to learn to pray. That is my biggest need as I face my situation."

When she finished speaking, though, the seminarians must have thought they should take lessons from her. She explained how, before the coming of missionaries to Hawaii, her people would sit outside their temples to meditate and prepare themselves to enter. Only after a long while did they dare creep to the altar to offer their petition. Then they would once again sit for a long time outside, this time to "breathe life" into their prayers.

How puzzled they were when the Christians came. The white people just "got up, uttered a few sentences, said Amen and were done." That's why Christians were given the name *haoles*, "without breath," a fitting epithet for people who don't breathe life into their prayers.[5]

One wonders who needed to be learning how to pray from whom. Both Christians and Hawaiians may be correct, however. There are times when prayer requires meditation, preparation, and recollection, as in the Hawaiian style. At other times briefer, more to the point prayers are in order.[6] In fact, we must pray like that often if we are to "pray without ceasing," as Paul urges us to do (1 Thessalonians 5:17, KJV).

The good news of the gospel is that, through Christ, all people now have gained privileged "access to the Father by one Spirit" (Ephesians 2:18). And the Spirit helps us when we pray, whether slowly or in haste. A steady practice of only hasty prayers, though, leaves us wanting (and needing) more. E. Stanley Jones's advice for making the prayer hour effective is to be recommended.

1. Have the prayer hour and build your life around it. Make things fit into it, not it into things.

2. At first be silent, letting your mind relax and roam across your life to see whether it stops at anything wrong. If so, tell God you will right it.

3. Bathe your thought in His Word. It will wash the dust from your eyes.

4. Write down what comes to you as you pore over His Word.

5. Take obedience with you into that hour, for you will know as much of God, and only as much of God, as you are willing to put into practice! For God will answer many of your prayers—through you.[7]

God Understands

It is evident by now, isn't it, that effectiveness in prayer does not depend on eloquence, on any charms or rituals or magic, on personal worthiness before God, on any stipulated place or length of time, or any kind of virtue we offer on our knees. We can pray with confidence only because "the Spirit helps us," and because He does, God, "who searches our hearts [and] knows the mind of the Spirit," intercedes for us.

In this chapter, I've quoted the learned theologian, Helmut Thielicke. I don't want to mislead, however. I quoted him because he was saying something helpful, not because of great learning that might somehow make him more advanced in prayer than the humble peasant on his knees. Theological studies don't contribute much to skill in prayer. Neither theologian nor peasant, Corrie ten Boom has helped me as much as anyone has. Her child-like faith and hopeful prayers sustained her from the security of her father's home through the horrors of the Nazi Holocaust to the peace and fame of her old age.

In one of her meditations, Miss ten Boom recalls when she was a little girl, her father used to tuck her in bed, talking and praying with her. He would lay his big hand on her little face; she wouldn't move because she wanted to keep the feeling of his hand there. It comforted her.

Years later, when a prisoner in a concentration camp, she would pray as a grown woman with the trust of the little child, "My heavenly Father, will you lay Your hand on my face?" That simple prayer would bring her peace, and she could sleep.[8]

She placed herself in His hands, and knew He understood.

Hers was the trust of Jesus on the cross, who knew His Father understood and would take care of Him. "Father, into your hands I commit my spirit" (Luke 23:46).

Dr. Paul Tournier comments on the varieties of prayers we offer. Prayer may be

—"moments of silent adoration which constitute supreme fellowship with God."

—"a dialogue, even though it may not be put into thoughts and sentences."

—"sudden moments of joy that are more binding than promises."

—"heart-rending cries that ring truer than praises learned by rote."

—"liturgical prayers, repeated since childhood, into which one so puts one's heart that they are more personal than extempore prayers that strain after originality."[9]

We are tempted to place these prayers on a scale, grading them, making certain that our kind of prayer gets the top score. But Dr. Tournier rightly insists "our own personal experience can never be taken as the norm for other people." Neither can our temperament. Intuitive, logical, intellectual, and emotional personalities will approach God in terms dictated by temperament, he affirms, and I hasten to agree with him.

The joy is that God understands them all.

As this chapter comes to a close, what could be more appropriate than right now, as you are, who you are, with your own peculiar temperament, talk to God.

Praise Him.
Confess to Him.
Give Him thanks for hearing and understanding.
Ask Him into your heart.
Invite Him to ride through life with you.
Let Him drive.

Lord, what a change within us one short hour
Spent in Thy presence will prevail to make!
What heavy burdens from our bosoms take,
What parched grounds refresh as with a shower!
We kneel, and all around us seems to lower;
We rise, and all, the distant and the near,
Stands forth in sunny outline brave and clear;
We kneel, how weak! we rise, how full of power!
Why, therefore, should we do ourselves this wrong,
Or others, that we are not always strong,
That we are ever overborne with care,
That we should ever weak or heartless be,
Anxious or troubled, when with us is prayer,
And joy and strength and courage are with Thee![10]

Notes

[1]This quotation, clipped from a church paper, was given to me many years ago. I cannot name Dr. Carrel's work from which this excerpt comes. (Italics mine.)

[2]Zora Neale Hurston, *Journal of American Folklore*, 44:174, 1932.

[3]Tom Sine, *The Mustard Seed Conspiracy* (Waco: Word Books, 1981), p. 139.

[4]John W. Doberstein, editor and translator, *Christ and the Meaning of Life: A Book of Sermons and Meditations* (Grand Rapids: Baker Book House, 1962), pp. 90, 91.

[5]Robert J. McCracken, *Putting Faith to Work* (Carmel, New York: Guideposts Associates, 1960), p. 181.

[6]Like the time during one of Dwight L. Moody's campaigns when a minister offered an unusually long prayer. Moody broke in to tell the congregation, "While that good brother is finishing his prayer, we'll sing a hymn" (Leslie B. Flynn, *Serve Him With Mirth*, p. 69).

[7]E. Stanley Jones, *Victorious Living* (New York: Abingdon Press, 1936), p. 253.

[8]Corrie ten Boom, *Each New Day* (Old Tappan, New Jersey: Fleming H. Revell Company, 1977), p. 114.

[9]Dr. Paul Tournier, *The Meaning of Persons* (New York: Harper and Row, 1957), p. 166.

[10]Richard Chenevix Trench, 1807-1886.

9

THE STRONGEST PERSON IN THE NEIGHBORHOOD

Luke 10:25-37

In one arena of life — the most important — the weak and the strong are equal. It has been given to all persons, of whatever race or religion or socio-economic or physical condition, to be able to do the one thing most necessary to a complete life, the one thing the very doing of which gives strength to the doer: loving one's neighbor.

The lesson is taught in the most famous of all Jesus' stories, the Parable of the Good Samaritan, a story so well, so often repeated out of context, that few people know why Jesus told it in the first place. Reading it in the Bible, we are surprised to discover Jesus used it to illustrate His answer to a question about getting ready for Heaven.

On one occasion an expert in the law stood up to test Jesus, "Teacher," he asked, "what must I do to inherit eternal life?"

"What is written in the Law?" he replied, "How do you read it?"

He answered: "'Love the Lord your God with all your heart and with all your soul and with all your strength and with all your mind'; and, 'Love your neighbor as yourself.'"

"You have answered correctly," Jesus replied. "Do this and you will live."

But he wanted to justify himself, so he asked Jesus, "And who is my neighbor?" (Luke 10:25-29).

Jesus' response to the lawyer's follow-up question is the parable.

You can see why it appeals to Doctor Luke. You can't fool physicians; they know that under our clothes and cosmetics we are basically about the same. We like to distinguish ourselves from the common herd by our status symbols, but we can't deny the truth: regardless of apparent racial or religious differences, one human being is put together pretty much the way every other one is. And on the Day of Judgment, our coiffures and costumes won't be much value to us. The Lord's queries are going to make us squirm. They won't be about where we bought our clothes or how we climbed the corporate ladder. They will have to do with how we treated our neighbors—all of our neighbors.

Forever Is Now

The encounter begins with a question about eternity: "What must I do to inherit eternal life?" Jesus has a way of turning such a question back into the present. He has a question of His own: "What are you doing now?" For Him, time stands at the threshold of forever. We prefer thinking in two separate categories—time and eternity. But time is in eternity, hence our timely acts have everlasting consequences.

Death is not one of our favorite subjects of conversation. We are like a successful businessman I read about. A younger man was dining with him. After dinner he turned to his host and asked whether he believed in personal immortality. The man said, "Of course, I believe in Heaven and eternal bliss; but I do wish you wouldn't start such an unpleasant topic."[1]

It isn't a pleasant subject, is it, especially when you're in the prime of life? It's certainly not a dominant subject; we push it aside to attend more immediate, relevant concerns. It does become more compelling as we grow older, with desires yet unfulfilled, more than we can fit into our remaining years. We don't want to quit. We hope for eternity, where we hope to keep going and doing.

In some circles, it has become socially unacceptable to discuss death—I mean discuss it earnestly, seeking its meaning, probing its impact on life. That old conversational taboo, sex, has been replaced by death. Don't even use the word. It's too unpleasant.

For a Christian, however, it isn't an unsavory topic at all. The Scriptures give us every reason to look upon our dying without fear. Further, it's comforting to believe our lives don't stop here, with a grave. We seek more. We desire to be forever with those we love. We are intrigued by the prospects.

Fascination with the subject isn't good enough, though. We have to do something about here and now. As Susan Ertz has pointedly observed, "Millions long for immortality who do not know what to do with themselves on a rainy Sunday afternoon."[2] They might be better occupied, Jesus' story implies, if they were out giving a hand to their neighbors.

Jesus has nothing directly to say about the legal expert's topic. Instead He turns the man's eyes from far off paradise to nearby needy human beings. Norman Cousins, coming from a different perspective, ends up at the same place: "We may not be able to unravel the ultimate mystery of life but one thing is certainly within our capacity: We can do a better job of caring for human life than we are now doing."[3]

This observation is exactly the point of Jesus' parable. The lawyer assumes that there is life after death, and that there is a way to prepare for it. This second concern prompts Jesus' story. To prepare to live forever with a loving God, one must learn to love with a love like His.

Neighborhood Is Wherever

It's far more popular to speculate about Heaven than to help your neighbor. The religious lawyer already knows he is supposed to love his neighbor; as a good student of the Law of Moses, he didn't need a review of Leviticus 19:18. Has he obeyed it? We suspect not, since Luke says "he wanted to justify himself." He needs a loophole. He thinks he has found it: "And who is my neighbor?" His case rests on Jesus' definition of the word.

But Jesus doesn't define; He launches His tale (Luke 10:30-37). "A man was going down from Jerusalem to Jericho. . . ." Not a long but a treacherous journey dotted with a number of ambush sites. Travel was treacherous business in those days. Jesus doesn't tell us the traveler is a Jew, a fellow countryman. We assume it. His benefactor's race is explicitly given: "But a Samaritan. . . ." A hated Samaritan, excluded by race and religion from Jews, who thought themselves pure, the people of God.

As He finishes His story, Jesus asks, "Which of these three do you think was a neighbor to the man who fell into the hands of robbers?" (Luke 10:36). He asks the question to force the truth from the legal expert. How His final words then must have stung: "Go and do likewise."

We can't read the story disinterestedly. The parable won't leave our consciences alone. We have neighbors, too. And we would take care of them, we protest, if we had the means. It's just that, well, you understand, we don't have any extra money; and every minute of our time is taken; and we aren't very strong; and besides, that's the job of the government or of rich people.

Which sounds very good, except that governments and rich people don't do it very well, either. One lesson I learned early in life is that, for the most part (there are some wonderful exceptions), rich people got to be rich by keeping their money. They take; they don't give.

Phyllis McGinley's little poem, "The Old Philanthropist," captures the problem:

His millions make museums bright;
Harvard anticipates his will;

While his young typist weeps at night
Over a druggist's bill.[4]

The old philanthropist isn't exactly uncharitable. No, he gives generously — where his gift will be noticed. Where he'll get proper credit. The typist? Well, he gets his wages. He must learn to manage.

In one of his books, Dr. Paul Tournier quotes a comment he must have heard frequently: "I could never be a doctor. I can't bear seeing people suffer." His answer is the only possible one:

> I think the best doctors are those who cannot bear to see suffering, and who try to bring relief and healing in spite of the limitations of our means, and who pursue their vocation in spite of the suffering it imposes on them.[5]

It's the ones who can't stand it who do something about it. People who "can't bear seeing people suffer" are in fact bearing it very well.

What they need is a touch of the spirit of Sir Philip Sidney, the sixteenth century British poet who, when he was fatally wounded at the Battle of Zutphen, handed his cup of water to an equally wounded comrade with the words, "Thy necessity is yet greater than mine." Then he died.

The greater necessity is what defines the neighbor. Inability to tolerate suffering in another is what compels compassion. Good neighbors cannot, will not, allow themselves to become calloused against someone's need, so they do what they can, where they are, to ease the pain. They are as different as they can be from the nineteenth-century philosopher Nietzsche, who grumped, "Beggars should be abolished. It annoys one to give to them and it annoys one not to give to them." Nietzsche's solution is simple: do away with them!

Hardly a Christian resolution to the problem.

Another approach is far better. Somebody who enjoys statistics said that if you just do one act of kindness to somebody every day for forty years, you will have made 14,600 people happy for at least a little while. Only one deed a day. For some reason, though, this seems an awfully high expectation, doesn't it? We've been taught to look out for ourselves. The world owes us the kindness. We've got to get what's coming to us. Such is the wisdom of the streets. Then we go to church, and the minister says something our ears cannot hear. We hardly know what to do with the Parable of the Good Samaritan. Like the lawyer, we scramble to find a loophole. Surely Jesus doesn't mean us, does He?

Do you know this prayer? Could you pray this prayer?

> Teach me to feel another's woe,
> To hide the fault I see
> That mercy I to others show,
> That mercy show to me.[6]

Would we dare — could we dare — to ask that we be treated as mercifully as we treat others? To have done to us what we have done to others? It's a courageous prayer, isn't it?

A few years ago, my good friend Ted Yamamori, who heads Food for the Hungry, invited me along on one of his periodic visits to Ethiopia. We went in the midst of a severe famine. We flew from Addis Ababa, the capital, into the mountains to Gondar, twelve thousand feet high, a distribution point from which food was taken by truck and pack animals into the remote mountainous regions of northern Ethiopia.

Ever since that visit, I've been concerned about the nation, devouring newspaper and magazine articles to see what has been happening to those hurting people I met. The civil war between Eritrea and the central government of Ethiopia seems to go on without end. I was

110

horrified a couple years after our visit to learn that Food for the Hungry had been driven out of Gondar. Ted said the war had forced out the relief workers, and the soldiers had confiscated all the grain and other foodstuffs at the center.

My mind once more pictured those hundreds and thousands of people I saw in Ethiopia, emaciated, bloated, dying. To think that now nobody would be able to get food into that area, and that many of the people I saw would starve—my mind fought the facts. Yet, there was another fact even more maddening. It was the statement of a United Nations relief official, quoted in a magazine below a picture of starving Ethiopian children. "I have yet to see a soldier on either side who is hungry."[7]

The children starve. But the war must go on. Where is mercy?

Where is the neighbor?

Jesus' parable says your neighborhood is where you are, where you work, where you live, where you play, where you vacation, the community you drive through, those places you go out of your way to find. Where there is need. Where you can feel the suffering. And where you can make a difference to the sufferer.

A recent article on the distinction between males and females didn't make me very happy, either. I'm not yet sure the author persuaded me. The thesis was that physiologically women are better equipped to be sensitive to the sufferings of others than men are. Something changes in the fetus stage that leaves males without the intuitive sensitivity of women.

Hmmmm, I don't know. I do know, though, that in this parable Jesus is speaking as a man to men about men. He takes it for granted that even men can feel the hurt of a robbery and assault victim. Even a man can turn aside from a hurried business trip to pour oil and wine on the victim and find him lodging and pay his bills. Even a man can feel for his neighbor.

The Nobel Prize novelist Isaac Singer was asked one time why he was a vegetarian. Was he doing it for his health? I love his answer. He said, "I did not become a vegetarian for my health. I did it for the health of the chickens."[8] I confess I seldom look at my meals from the viewpoint of the chicken—or the steer or the fish. How far I want to push this reasoning I don't know. I have to push it this far in my dealings with humans, at least: I must avoid anything that forces suffering on another, and must do whatever I can to ease hurts wherever I find them. My neighborhood is wherever I happen to be at the moment. And my neighbor is anybody within my reach who has a need.

"Religion" Is Not Enough

The surprising aspect of this incident to those of us who have spent our lives in church is what Jesus does not say. The man asks a question about eternal life, and Jesus absolutely ignores religion, except to employ a couple of religious leaders as bad examples. Of course, Jesus is taking the man's expertise in religious law for granted, but still, isn't it strange that He doesn't tell him something "religious" to do?

I am making the same assumption Jesus makes as I write to you. I'm taking for granted the religious interest of anyone who would bother to read a Bible study book like this one. Someone with no interest in religion would have given up in boredom long before reaching this chapter. So I'm safely assuming you, as I, are well acquainted with the proper religious duties and doctrines. We are faithful in observing the Christian faith's distinctive rites. We can be counted on to be in the Lord's house on the Lord's Day.

In other words, we're the good ones.

Are you struggling, as I am, with the suspicion that Jesus would still say to us, "That's not yet enough. What are you doing for your neighbor?"

The priest and the Levite are specifically mentioned in the parable. That bothers me, because I am the Christian equivalent of one of them, a "religious leader." Even worse, I identify with their behavior. They walk by the man. They're running very big operations and their calendars are full and they have meetings to go to and speeches to make and appearances to show up for and other people to take care of. You can understand why they don't have time to stop. They are busy people. Very important people. Very blind people.

Tony Campolo's stories disturb me almost as much as some of Jesus'. This latter-day prophet hits you where you live. One of them, of his visit to a retirement home, I cannot get out of my mind. My mother lives in one. I don't get to see her often because of the twelve hundred miles between us. The visiting chaplain there shocked me when he said most nursing home residents never receive a visit of any kind from anyone. They are abandoned.

On his visit, Campolo went through the roster of residents and noticed the name of a lady who hadn't been visited for eighteen months. He made his way through the clean, well-kept wards to her bed, one of twenty in her large ward. He tried to start a conversation but didn't get very far. He was distracted by a nurse who came in to feed the patients. She went to the first bed and pried open the mouth of the elderly woman, shoved food in and ordered, "Swallow it." She repeated the process five times.

Campolo couldn't stand it. Indignantly he asked her, "Do you have to do it that way?" She turned to him and said, "You're a minister, aren't you?"

"Yes, how did you know?"

"Your kind is always coming in here complaining about the things I do. Mister, I have forty patients to feed in an hour. I wish I could be gentle, but the limitation on my time forces me to do things in a very unpleasant manner." She told him if he was so concerned about how these women were eating, he should get the women's group of his church to spend a day a week giving them lunch. It would probably be a better use of their time than whatever they were doing now.

It sounded like a good idea, so he went back to his church, presented the proposal to the ladies, and they refused. They said they would rather roll bandages for Africa.[9]

Of course, they would! It's always easier to be concerned at a safe distance. Where we don't get our hands dirty. Where we don't have to deal with unpleasantries like smelly nursing homes and helpless old people. Where we don't have to inconvenience ourselves.

A very busy minister was on the verge of a breakdown, under terrible stress. He asked the people of his church if they would help to unload him just a little bit. After the announcement was made to the church, a couple of university students came up to ask him if there was a time during the week when the two of them could meet with him to pray for more time to relax. Their offer offended him. He didn't need their prayer. He needed them to leave him alone.[10]

They meant well, but they just weren't being sensitive to the man's need. What makes real empathy for others difficult is that it requires taking the attention off ourselves entirely and fixing it on them. It means meeting others' needs according to their wants, not ours.

I usually like Dag Hammarskjold's maxims, but when he says, "goodness is something so simple: always to live for others, never to seek one's own advantage,"[11] I have to take issue with him. His description of goodness is correct; his assessment that it's easy to achieve is not.

I was also disturbed by something that Leslie Weatherhead wrote. The famous World War II London preacher told of a letter he once received from a policeman, who said that he had been a policeman for twenty-five years, thirteen of them in London's East End — a tough district. Never once in all those years had he met a Christian laboring among the real down-and-out people late at night or in the early hours. He said on the other hand he had often seen a poor bedraggled prostitute feeding a poor derelict at a coffee stall, not in any hope of gain but out of sheer pity and goodness of heart. "No wonder Jesus has a kind word and a promise for them."[12]

No wonder. Why do I use an example of a prostitute feeding a derelict? Because I'm writing for very polite persons who have no use for prostitution and who probably are a little put off that I would use such a person as an example of goodness. If so, we are feeling something of the sting that pricked the lawyer by the time Jesus finished His story of a despised Samaritan. How could He speak so warmly of a social pariah? The lawyer and his fellow listeners were of the People of God, strong in their religion, pious of the pious, best of the best. All their lives they had looked down on inferior Samaritans as people of impure religion and impure lives.

My guess is they walked away from Jesus grumbling.

If you think this was a passing fancy of Jesus', may I recommend another of His stories, this one also dealing with Heaven and how to get there? It's found in Matthew 25. We call it the Parable of the Sheep and the Goats.

Once again, religion isn't the criterion for entry into Paradise. Old-fashioned, non-sectarian charity is. You don't have to be strong in religion to practice it.

I recently spent a little time with an old and dear friend. We drove to lunch together in his shiny new red Corvette. He offered to let me drive. I was afraid to. It was out of my league. He is very successful, but as I went away from our conversation, I realized we hadn't once given thought to the sick or the hungry or the imprisoned or the naked. Not once. Oh, it was just a conversation between a couple of old friends, and it might have introduced a discordant note to talk about our needy neighbors. But I left that conversation to work on this book, and I wished I could have reported on our concern for the plight of our neighbors.

Compared to me, my friend is rich. Monetarily speaking, he is the strong one and I am weak. But that day, we were equally weak, equally self-centered. The measure of your financial strength is not in what you've accumulated, but in what you feel you can afford to give away. It isn't what you have that counts, but what you do with it. By that standard, we were paupers.

It's not too late for us. Both of us still can become good neighbors, if we want to.

Only if we do will we become strong.

Notes

[1]Geoffrey Faber, *Oxford Apostles* (London: Faber and Faber, 1974), pp. 161, 162.

[2]Jon Winokur, compiler, *The Portable Curmudgeon* (New York: New American Library, 1987), p. 154.

[3]Norman Cousins, *Human Options* (New York and London: W. W. Norton and Company, 1981), p. 206.

[4]"Gallery of Elders," copyright 1953 by Phyllis McGinley, renewed © 1981 by Phyllis Hayden Blake. From *Times Three* by Phyllis McGinley. Used by permission of Viking Penguin, a division of Penguin Books USA Inc.

[5]Dr. Paul Tournier, *A Doctor's Casebook* (New York: Harper and Row, 1960), p. 176.

[6]Alexander Pope, "The Universal Prayer."

[7]"Images '86," *Time*, December 29, 1986, pp. 44, 45.

[8]*Time*, January 2, 1984, p. 79.

[9]Tony Campolo, *The Success Fantasy* (Wheaton: Victor Books, 1960), pp. 129-131.

[10]Jim Conway, *The Midlife Crisis* (Elgin, IL: Cook Publishing, 1978), p. 54.

[11]Leif Sjoberg and W. H. Auden, translators, *Markings* (New York: Alfred A. Knopf, 1964), p. 89.

[12]Leslie Weatherhead, *When the Lamp Flickers* (Nashville: Abingdon-Cokesbury Press, 1948), p. 39.

10

Strong Enough to Say You're Sorry

John 21:1-19

An unsuspected source of strength in weakness is repentance. I learned a lot about it in my home church, but the stress was usually on its relation to conversion. We were taught a five-finger exercise in Sunday school to help us remember the "steps of salvation." Each finger stood for a step: faith, repentance, confession, baptism, and leading the Christian life. Later, I learned another version. The first three fingers stood for the believer's role in conversion: faith, repentance, and baptism. The last two were for what God gives us: remission of sins and the gift of the Holy Spirit.

These useful memory tools have lasted me a lifetime. Less helpful, however, has been my tendency to leave repentance at conversion without perceiving its crucial role in a person's Christian walk and enjoyment of God's love. Lacking a healthy respect for it, we can't fully appropriate that "strength not our own."

Having fought his tempestuous personality all his life, the apostle Peter has had opportunity to learn to admit he is wrong and is humble enough to accept the grace that enables him to grow stronger in the Lord.

How Repenting Leads to Strength

We don't need to review the scandal of Peter's denial of Jesus. It's too well known to have to be retold here.[1]

Throughout the synoptic gospels (Matthew, Mark, and Luke), Peter's dominating figure looms larger than anyone else except Jesus. A strong natural leader, Peter must have ranked first among the disciples as soon as the group was formed. Bold to the point of recklessness, outspoken to the brink of rudeness, dynamic, honest, and eager to learn, Peter seemed the ideal lieutenant for Jesus. Then came Jesus' arrest, then His rigged trial, then Peter's explosive denial.

What didn't follow is what saved Peter. Once he had perpetrated the appalling sin, he didn't become defensive or try to rationalize his behavior. He didn't blame Jesus. He didn't pretend he had acted in ignorance. He didn't use any of the devices we almost automatically employ to put the best face on our worst conduct. Instead, "he went outside and wept bitterly" (Matthew 26:75).

Peter's tears were more than remorse. Remorse drives people apart, but Peter stayed with his friends. And in a fishing trip he organized some days later, we glimpse an important clue to his character. As John tells the events of Christ's final days on earth, when Peter and his fishing buddies become aware it is Jesus who is shouting to them, Peter is the first one to rush up to greet Him.

At first, this may not seem significant. Peter's always at the head of the line. He organized this fishing party. Being in charge and being first is just what Peter does best.

Here, however, the circumstances are different. He's dealing with the man he denied. A person's natural instinct, when he has wronged someone else, is to draw away. This is undoubtedly why the angel instructed the three woman at Jesus' tomb to "go, tell his disciples *and Peter* [specifically], 'He is going ahead of you into Galilee'" (Mark 16:7). It is a signal to Peter that, in spite of his heinous deed, the Lord has not given up on him. (Jesus' unwavering love for His disciples — and for us — is why I entitled one of my earlier books *The Lord of Love*. Loving us is what *He* does best!)

So Peter has reason to hope everything will be all right between them. Yet some doubt must have gnawed at him. Peter's sin was enormous. To deny your best friend in His greatest crisis is as offensive as Judas' turning Jesus over to the authorities for a fistful of money.

But Peter doesn't hesitate to greet his Lord. He doesn't have to say anything more; his body language is eloquent. The repentance that first expressed itself in tears on the night of Jesus' trial now declares itself in his running to Jesus on shore. Peter hasn't rejected his Lord. He has instead turned his spiritual setback into an experience of renewal.

At the trial, immediately after Peter shouted, "I don't know what you're talking about," when he was accused of associating with Jesus, "the Lord turned and looked straight at Peter." It was then that Peter "went outside and wept bitterly" (Luke 22:60-62). How that look must have kept on piercing his conscience all the time between the crucifixion and this reunion on the shores of Galilee.

But now reconciliation is possible. All Peter's defenses and pretensions are gone. "There is in repentance this beautiful mystery—that we may fly fastest home on broken wing."[2] Peter has come "home."

Bruce Larson discovered the importance of living without pretense when he was an infantry recruit at Fort Benning, Georgia. The lesson to be learned was grits. Sitting at his first breakfast at his mess hall table with ten other men, he scooped up a large helping of what looked like cream of wheat. He added milk and sugar. A tall mountain boy watching bug-eyed from across the table asked him, "Is that the way you eat grits?"

Larson was from Chicago. He wasn't about to admit he'd never seen grits in his life. "Oh, yes. This is how we eat grits in Chicago," he lied. Then he had to eat the terrible tasting concoction. He watched with envy as his table mate added butter and salt and pepper, which is the "proper" way to eat grits. But a few days later, when grits were again the treat of the morning and when the mountaineer was once again at his table, he helped himself to another bowl, poured milk and sugar on them — and forced the mess down.

Larson's reason for telling the story on himself (and mine in repeating it) is to warn of the grave consequences of denying our sins (or even our ignorance). "We do not want to admit our mistakes. We would rather go to hell maintaining our innocence than to say, 'I was wrong.'"[3] So we remain on the defensive and out of the inner circle of fellowship. Relationships are built on honesty and trust, not pretense and defense.

Reconciliation with Jesus is possible for Peter because he doesn't compound denial with denial. He was guilty of repudiating Jesus in the first place, but he is not now guilty of denying his denial. His tears were genuine; his joy now in the presence of Jesus is transparent.

He can relish the moment because his heart has prepared for it through honest repentance. His "broken wing" has brought him to the healer of broken wings . . . and hearts. The healer is ever ready to help the penitent.

The role of repentance in heart preparation is often underestimated. You would have no trouble telling anyone what Jesus' great commandment is. Every disciple of Jesus knows He summarized the entire law in one twofold command: to love God with all your being, and to love your neighbor as yourself (Mark 12:28-31). What is not so well known is that long before Jesus commanded us to love He commanded us to repent. He opened His ministry echoing the vital words of John the Baptist: "The time has come. . . . The kingdom of God is near. Repent and believe the good news!" (Mark 1:15). Not only love, but even genuine belief, isn't possible without a change of heart. Repentance is what changes it.

I smiled when I read this reference to repentance in Garrison Keillor's *We Are Still Married*. The humorist quotes a letter of the fictional Clarence Bunsen to his wife

Arlene from Saskatchewan, where he's fishing in forty-six-degrees-below-zero weather. He thinks a lot while holding his line. He could think at home, of course, but he couldn't spit there. He needs to think, he says, because

> a man needs to contemplate his sins and decide which ones to repent of and which to be more patient with and see if they might not cure themselves. Women don't need this because women are better than men.[4]

It's a fine plan, except it doesn't work. Sins just don't cure themselves. If you harbor a grudge or nurse a bitterness or carry the memory of a wrong you did (which is at least as damaging as the memory of a wrong done you), you have no choice. For your sake. And (sorry, Clarence) you can't pick and choose. You can't cleanse part of your heart. Patience is a virtue, but patience with your sins against others is deadly. It's the sin of Adolph Eichman, one of Hitler's cruelest comrades, who insisted at his trial he had nothing to regret and would not repent. "Repentance is for little children," he huffed.[5]

He was telling a greater truth than he knew. Jesus contended we couldn't enter the kingdom of Heaven unless we turn and become like children. If repenting is what children do (and it is), so be it. It is what adults must do, too. Without it, all is lost: all hope of Heaven, all hope of lasting relationships on earth.

But when repentance is real and total, then you enter into the bliss enjoyed only by persons who have nothing left to hide. Such persons need no defenses, make no excuses, offer no rationalizations, and are capable of rich and lasting relationships. In such open relationships (with God, with our "neighbors") strength is found.

How Service Confirms Repentance

John the Baptist charged the Pharisees to "produce fruit in keeping with repentance" (Matthew 3:8). Paul told

King Agrippa the goal of his preaching was "that they should repent and turn to God and prove their repentance by their deeds" (Acts 26:20). In writing to the Corinthians, Paul spelled out some healthy consequences of genuine sorrow:

> Godly sorrow brings repentance that leads to salvation and leaves no regret, but worldly sorrow brings death. See what this godly sorrow has produced in you: what earnestness, what eagerness to clear yourselves, what indignation, what alarm, what longing, what concern, what readiness to see justice done (2 Corinthians 7:10, 11).

The repentance that clears one's heart and makes it ready for relationship is confirmed not only in words ("I'm sorry") but more importantly in actions. This is why Jesus three times (once for each of Peter's denials) asks him with growing intensity, "Peter, do you love me?"

Each time Peter affirms his love, the last time with consternation.

To each of Peter's declarations of love Jesus attaches an assignment: "Feed my sheep" (John 21:15-17). "I believe your words, Peter. But you spoke words to Me before. Good words, loving words. Words you meant. But when the test came, you crumbled. You need to offer more than words, Peter. You need to show Me. Feed my sheep."

This is still the charge to today's believers, individually and in church life. Churches like to gather in national conventions and deliberate on somebody's latest proposals for curing the nation's ills. They pass resolutions instructing governments and individuals what to do about housing and international relations and the economy and crime and abortion and homosexuality and women's and children's rights and a myriad of other social problems. They are experts in passing resolutions. It's a relatively easy expertise to acquire. It's far easier to convene and converse and resolve than it is to feed sheep. For all our talk, however, we individual believers remain estranged from one another, unreconciled to God or to humanity.

Because we haven't repented, we aren't doing the deeds of repentance. The result is weak churches and weak Christians. Evil hearts can be changed and society's ills can best be addressed by men and women who follow up their conversions by keeping on with deeds befitting their repentance. Dame Julian of England said, "The most painful thing a soul can do is to turn from God through sin." And Philip Toynbee added, "And the second most painful thing a soul can do is to turn from sin to God."[6]

Painful, because it is difficult to face God.

Painful, because it is difficult to face oneself.

Painful, because it is hard to let God remake us into His image.

Painful, because defending and denying is more natural than confessing and loving and feeding His sheep.

The pain is exposed in a prayer in T. S. Eliot's play, *Murder in the Cathedral*:

Forgive us, O Lord, we acknowledge ourselves as types of the common man,

Of the men and women who shut the door and sit by the fire;

Who fear the blessing of God, the loneliness of the night of God, the surrender required.[7]

We don't repent because we are afraid of the consequences. Because we don't repent, we shut ourselves in and take care of our own creature comforts. Because we don't do the deeds of repentance, we grow weaker. Duped into believing we are strong enough to go it alone, we won't avail ourselves of strength we must have.

There's a Newark, Ohio, native I'd like to meet who finally did something about his bad conscience. According to our town newspaper, in 1986 he cleared up a very old debt. The city parks department received his

$1400 check to pay for some vandalism he perpetrated thirty-five years earlier. He figured he did about one hundred dollars' worth of damage, but he paid interest. He signed his note, "An ex-mischievous kid. Thanks for your patience."[8] Thirty-five years is a long time to have something on your conscience. He had most certainly repented years earlier. Finally, he did something about it. At the time it seemed a small misdemeanor. It just never went away; and it wouldn't, until he had the integrity to pay.

A friend of mine spent some time in prison to pay for some poor business judgment. Fully accepting the blame for his actions, he was later able to call his year there the richest in his life. He wrote a series of letters from prison to his daughter. I am helped by his insights in these published letters. One thing missing in prison, he said, was any sense of personal guilt on the part of most of the inmates.

> Since all are thrust into Classification without regard to age, background, accusation, race, etc., obviously it represents every imaginable description of human being. My observation is that of the 142 men in the room in which I was confined, there was not one who did not feel that he had been wronged in being sent to prison. In other words, if you depend on each man's evaluation of his own situation, there were no guilty men.[9]

Nevertheless, more objective judges found them guilty.

Most guilty persons are never sent to jail, but they live in prisons of their own constructing, penned up, defensive, weakened by their refusal to repent. Unrepentant, they are unwilling to serve people; as a result they are forced to serve time.

Jesus' questions are explicit: "Peter, do you love me?" If Peter does, and he does, then he must show that love not in doing something special for the Lord, some sacrifice or oblation or other act of worship, but in doing something for the sheep. There's nothing in it for Jesus.

We have a crude saying in the English language that parallels this: "Love me, love my dog." If you say you love me, even my dog will know it. If you say you love me, you will love the ones whom I love. You don't love me at all if you love only me.

Although my wife makes fun of me, I am a crossword puzzle addict. I work them because I like them. You learn interesting things and you increase your vocabulary by a lot, although there are few places to use your new words except in crossword puzzles, which is why you have to keep buying more. A recent puzzle had a little theology lesson in it. The clue to 51 across was "amend one's life." The correct word was "repent."

That's exactly what I've been talking about! Until we "amend our lives," we remain weaker than we ought. And that amending is never strictly personal; it is interpersonal.

"Peter, do you love Me? Amend your life. Feed My sheep."

It's a lesson Nobuo Fujita understood. In September, 1942, Imperial Japanese Navy Pilot Fujita dropped incendiary bombs over Brookings, Oregon, the only community on mainland America to be bombed during the Second World War. He never forgot what he did.

Neither did Brookings. The people there refused to hold a grudge against the man who tried to set fire to their town. Instead, in 1962, the Junior Chamber of Commerce invited him to serve as honorary grand marshal of the town's azalea festival. They had forgiven him.

It wasn't quite enough.

Fujita had to do something for them. For twenty years, he saved around $10,000 so he could fly three Brookings high-school students to Japan where they would tour the country as his guests. It was his way of making amends.

I'm telling you all this in order to get to his final comment. "After they have toured Japan, the war will finally be over for me."[10]

125

Forty years after the bombing, he could finally let his mind rest.

One more thing I should mention. Fujita was once a prosperous businessman, but his business failed. That's why it took so many years for him to raise the money. When he began his project, he had little money; he was financially weakened. I suspect that without his goal of flying the students to Japan, he would have remained weak. My guess is that it was his desire to do something for Brookings that gave him the strength to rebuild.

"Peter, do you love me?"

"Feed my sheep."

It'll make you strong.

Notes

[1]But just in case the details are fuzzy, you can find the story in Matthew 26:47-75.

[2]William L. Sullivan, *Epigrams and Criticisms in Miniature,* quoted in Gerald Kennedy's *A Reader's Notebook* (New York: Harper and Brothers, 1953), p. 254.

[3]Bruce Larson, *Dare to Live Now* (Carmen, New York: Guideposts Associates, 1972), p. 187.

[4]Garrison Keillor, *We Are Still Married* (New York: Viking by Penguin, 1989), pp. 85, 86.

[5]Hanna Arendt, *Eichman in Jerusalem* (New York and England: Penguin Books, 1964), p. 24.

[6]Philip Toynbee, *End of a Journey* (London: Bloomsbury Pub., 1988), p. 207.

[7]Excerpt from *Murder in the Cathedral* by T. S. Eliot, copyright 1935 by Harcourt Brace Jovanovich, Inc. and renewed 1963 by T. S. Eliot, reprinted by permission of the publisher.

[8]Mesa *Tribune*, April 19, 1986.

[9]Owen Crouch, *Dear Lorna* (New York: Carlton Press, Inc.), p. 14.

[10]*Time*, July 15, 1985, p. 45.

11

WHAT A DIFFERENCE
A FUTURE MAKES

Revelation 21:1-4

I discovered what a difference the future makes when I was thirty-five. Heaven wasn't on my mind at the time, but the rapid passing of my earthly years was.

I've not been much given to melancholy, but when my thirty-fifth birthday came around, it hit hard. I was halfway to my Biblical three score and ten years, and only thirty years from retirement. That was a depressing thought. There was still so much I wanted to do with my life, so many projects unfinished or unstarted. Life would be over long before I would be ready to quit.

After a few days of moping, a life-changing truth struck me. I couldn't do anything about the number of the days of my life, but there was something I could do about the number of my working days. Neither of my professions (pastor and professor) required retirement at sixty-five. So I moved my projected retirement to eighty. That gave me fifteen more years, and I have been feeling younger ever since. And stronger.

An often overlooked source of strength for the weak is the future. Nothing is more defeating than believing you have nothing more to look forward to. I've often thought of that lady in Boston who came from an old New England family. She was the embodiment of self-satisfaction. When she was once asked why she never traveled, she replied, "Why should I? I'm already there!"

I'm not. And I suspect you aren't either, or you wouldn't be reading this book. You have places to go, people to see, and things to do. You need time. You need the future.

Tom Landry explains what an assured future did for him. After four years as the new coach of the brand new Dallas Cowboys, his team still hadn't posted a winning season. In fact, the 1963 season's 4-10 record was even worse than the year before. Fans were demanding Landry's head. Tex Schramm, general manager of the Cowboys, went to the owner, Clint Murchison, to talk about the criticism swirling around Landry.

"We have to do something about all this public criticism of Landry," Schramm told Murchison.

"That's easy enough," Clint replied. "We'll just give Tom a new ten-year contract. That ought to shut people up."[1] Since Landry still had a year to go on his original contract, that gave him an eleven-year commitment, unprecedented for any professional in any major-league sport. Landry had been handed a future—not one he deserved, since his record had been so miserable, but one that was more like grace, unmerited favor from a benevolent owner. He still had a losing fifth season and only a tying sixth season—but the rest is history. For twenty-nine years, he piloted the Cowboys, during many of those years the best professional football team in existence.

What if he hadn't been granted that future? Where would Tom Landry be today?

That's the difference a future makes.

The Bible's message holds the future ever before us. Even when we die, we still have a tomorrow to look forward to. Knowing this, we find the strength to endure whatever the present moment throws at us. Our inspiration is Jesus,

> the author and perfecter of our faith, who for the joy set before him endured the cross, scorning its shame, and sat

down at the right hand of the throne of God. [We] consider him who endured such opposition from sinful men, so that [we] will not grow weary and lose heart (Hebrews 12:2, 3).

The book of Revelation has always puzzled its readers. All those visions and warnings, so open to misinterpretation, so easily misunderstood. You and I may differ in our reading of specific passages, but about one promise the book is so clear no one can miss it: God has prepared for His people a triumphant future.

Revelation was sent to seven churches in the province of Asia to bolster their faith during a period of fierce persecution. John's revelation is from God, "to show his servants what must soon take place" (Revelation 1:1), orchestrated by "the Alpha and the Omega . . . who is, and who was, and who is to come, the Almighty" (Revelation 1:8). It's a message of encouragement to besieged saints. For the moment, Satan may appear to be winning the struggle between good and evil, but don't be afraid. God is still on His throne and the future Jesus went to prepare for us is ready and waiting. Take heart.

Among the most memorable visions is the one found in the twenty-first chapter. There John is granted a glimpse of God's tomorrow. It's the new Jerusalem, the city of the people of God.

The dominant word is *new*: "new" Heaven, "new" earth. The future is somewhat analogous to what we have known, but only somewhat. Here on earth we experience loneliness, alienation, mourning, crying, pain, death. But in Heaven, where everything will be new, God will dwell with us and we shall be His people, and for us "'there will be no more death or mourning or crying or pain, for the old order of things has passed away.' He who was seated on the throne said, 'I am making everything new!'"(Revelation 21:4, 5).

The implication is clear. Since what is to come is going to be so far superior to what we are experiencing now, we had better "hang in there," like Jesus "enduring the cross," so we can enjoy Heaven forever.

A good example of endurance is found in 2 Corinthians 4. Speaking of the message he preaches ("For we do not preach ourselves, but Jesus Christ as Lord, and ourselves as your servants for Jesus' sake," 2 Corinthians 4:5), Paul is at pains to give credit where credit is due. Just as his ministry is his only "through God's mercy" (2 Corinthians 4:1), so the strength to pursue his ministry is from God also: "But we have this treasure in jars of clay to show that this all-surpassing power is from God and not from us" (2 Corinthians 4:7).

God delivers this power to us in the midst of, not in place of, our conflicts. "We are hard pressed on every side, but not crushed; perplexed, but not in despair; persecuted, but not abandoned; struck down, but not destroyed" (2 Corinthians 4:8).

Paul may be attacked, pushed, confused, persecuted, and damaged, but he cannot be destroyed because, as John writes elsewhere, "the one who is in you is greater than the one who is in the world." Even if we should die, we don't fear, "because we know that the one who raised the Lord Jesus from the dead will also raise us with Jesus and present us with you in his presence" (2 Corinthians 4:14).

Body Crumbling or Spirit Renewing?

Elsewhere Paul catalogues the beating his body has taken:

Five times I received from the Jews the forty lashes minus one. Three times I was beaten with rods, once I was stoned, three times I was shipwrecked, I spent a night and a day in the open sea, I have been constantly on the move. I have been in danger from rivers, in danger from bandits, in danger from my own countrymen, in danger from Gentiles; in danger in the city, in danger in the country, in danger at sea;

and in danger from false brothers. I have labored and toiled and have often gone without sleep; I have known hunger and thirst and have often gone without food; I have been cold and naked. Besides everything else, I face daily the pressure of my concern for all the churches. Who is weak, and I do not feel weak? Who is led into sin, and I do not inwardly burn? (2 Corinthians 11:24-29).

Every time I read this list I wonder whether I could have endured what Paul went through for the sake of the ministry. He wasn't crushed. Why? What sustained him?

His answer is in 2 Corinthians 4:16: "Therefore we do not lose heart. Though outwardly we are wasting away, yet inwardly we are being renewed day by day."

His strength is an inner power, not dependent on the frailty of the flesh. That "jar of clay," his body, isn't much in itself. It isn't his only resource, however. Should something happen to it, not to worry:

Now we know that if the earthly tent we live in is destroyed, we have a building from God, an eternal house in heaven, not built by human hands. Meanwhile we groan, longing to be clothed with our heavenly dwelling, because when we are clothed, we will not be found naked. For while we are in this tent, we groan and are burdened, because we do not wish to be unclothed but to be clothed with our heavenly dwelling, so that what is mortal may be swallowed up by life (2 Corinthians 5:1-4).

So real is Paul's future existence with the Lord, he reserves the word *life* in this passage for what's to come.

Why aren't we worried? Because like Paul, "We live by faith, not by sight" (2 Corinthians 5:7). The reality ahead of us is greater than the perplexities around us, so we are drawn forward.

What strength of perseverance this faith gives us! One of the many lessons I have learned on this subject came back in the 1980s, when a friend of mine and I lost heavily in an investment. For me, the loss was extremely hard to accept, since I had borrowed the investment money (against my wife's better judgment). My friend lost even more money than I did. One day when we were consoling each other, I said, "Well, at least we have recovery time."

I was thinking of another friend, a man up in his retirement years, who had invested heavily in a speculative project. He withdrew his more conservatively deposited retirement funds to take a chance on a promise of much greater returns. His loss hurt more than mine because of his age. Time was against him. There was no way for him to recover the lost money. My younger friend and I would be all right. (As I write these words, the loan has been long since paid off. I did recover. And I had lost very little sleep during the recovery period because I knew time was on my side.) In the spate of books on Japanese management style flooding our bookstores since our chief Eastern competitors have been beating American companies so soundly, one key element in Japanese productivity has been reported again and again. While American CEOs keep their eyes glued to the quarterly bottom line on the profit/loss reports, their Japanese counterparts take a much longer view of things. They can endure temporary setbacks for the sake of long-term gains. Their farsightedness has helped them best their shortsighted American competitors on almost every front. They gain strength from the future.

This lesson was brought home to me by one of our church's staff members. Our Mike Prior and a ministerial colleague in another church were comparing the two churches' styles of operation. The colleague's church had a reputation for frequent staff changes. Apparently, the senior minister became impatient when his staff failed to meet his expectations. His method was to rid himself of the non-producer and replace him with another minister who, he hoped, would reach the senior man's goals.

Our church, to the contrary, has had a very stable staff with little turnover. "That doesn't mean we have always produced well," Mike explained. In fact, he said, "We all have had our bad years. We just hang on to each other until we get through them." We have been able to tough out those hard years together because we have felt secure in our jobs. Our church leaders want to hold the team together. From that security, we have all gained strength.

Paul applies this principle specifically to his physical stamina. His body is "wasting away"; his "earthly tent" is being destroyed by the erosion of years. Rather than despair, however, he exudes confidence. The future is his, whether in his present body or in his "building from God, an eternal house in heaven."

He has recovery time.

Christian leader John Haggai has passed on a lesson he learned from Bob Pierce, the exhuberant founder of World Vision. When Pierce was a young man, a respected minister gave him the secret behind winning organizations. "It's staying power," he said. Having made a careful study of leaders and organizations, biographies and autobiographies, history and contemporary leadership, the minister found staying power to be the one common element among the winners. Organizations whose leaders had higher education, greater reputation or natural gifts, or a greater network of relationships, would wither and die while others with fewer advantages achieved success.

> The latter simply exercised staying power. When they were hanging on the ledge, ready to crash into the abyss, fingers bleeding as their nails were pulled off from their fingers, the people who won were those who just kept clinging. Somehow, some way, God intervened; He honored their staying power and gave them deliverance.[2]

The minister's language is instructive, isn't it? They held on, until God intervened and gave them deliverance.

They had a future to realize; the God of the future helped them into it.

Momentary Troubles or Eternal Glory?

Christianity is future-oriented. Unlike so many schools of psychology, it does not believe we are what we are because of past conditioning. Our characters are not solely determined by our genes or childhood environment. A Christian is not driven by the past so much as drawn toward the future. The Christian faith is always hope-filled.

Power from the future helps us make today's decision. President Jimmy Carter's account of the Camp David Accord (between Israel and Egypt, initiated by America's President) includes the pivotal moment when Israel's stubborn, resistant Prime Minister Menachem Begin changed his mind. A vision of the future gave him the strength.

The discussions were deadlocked. Begin had rejected one of the major proposals crucial to any agreement. It appeared the conference was over.

As the three leaders were preparing to leave without an accord, Begin asked Carter to autograph some photographs of the three leaders (Begin, Carter, and Egypt's Anwar Sadat) for his eight grandchildren. Instead of merely signing his name, the President personally inscribed each of the eight sets with the individual grandchild's name before adding his signature. Then he carried them to Mr. Begin's cabin. He wanted to tell the Prime Minister he was sorry they had failed.

When Begin noticed the individualized inscriptions, he invited Mr. Carter into his cabin. As he looked at each grandchild's name, he said it aloud. He repeated this for all eight of them.

And by the time he was finished reading just the names of his grandchildren, his lip was trembling, and he had tears in his eyes. And we began to talk about the future of the world for our grandchildren if we didn't have peace. And we parted. I went back to my cabin.

In about fifteen minutes he sent word over that he had accepted the issue that he had previously rejected, and it was from there that we went on very quickly and concluded the agreement.[3]

What made the difference? The pull of the future. They had to come to an agreement for peace between Israel and Egypt for the sake of his grandchildren. Mr. Begin was acting out of a motive he had perhaps suppressed until that moment. When he pictured his own grandchildren living with the tensions and struggles that had marked his own life, he knew peace was not a luxury. It was a necessity. He had to do what he could to give it a chance.

Begin was applying the truth spoken by Elton Trueblood: "A man has made at least a start on discovering the meaning of human life when he plants shade trees under which he knows full well he will never sit."[4]

Such is the importance of the future.

Everything I have read on business or church or even personal leadership and management has been in agreement on this principle of drawing our strength from the future. George Deakin, for example, summarizes it this way: "A vision without a task makes a visionary; a task without a vision is drudgery; a vision with a task makes a missionary."[5]

The dynamic industrialist Henry Kaiser urges us to become very practical in our appropriation of the strength we can gain from a vision of our future: "Determine what you want more than anything else in life, write down the means by which you intend to attain it, and permit nothing to deter you from pursuing it."[6]

When Dwight Eisenhower was the president of Columbia University, he called John Erskine "the greatest teacher Columbia ever had." He was not alone in his admiration. Erskine's achievements in the areas of teaching, concert piano playing, writing (sixty books), and administration (head of Julliard School of Music) were legendary. His wife Helen attributed his achievements to his "defiant optimism." He excelled, she said, because of

> his own excitement for learning and his trust in the future. He often said to her, "Let's tell our young people that the best books are yet to be written; the best paintings have not yet been painted; the best governments are yet to be formed; the best is yet to be done by *them*."[7]

This challenge gave them something to strive for.

I have found their words helpful at every stage of my life. When I was a toddler, I looked forward to being big (or in my case, bigger). When in elementary school, I eagerly anticipated high school. In high school, I wanted to go to college. In college, to have a career. In my career, I still anticipate, wondering what the next turn of events will bring me.

A friend of mine has just retired. We're the same age. I'm still not ready. But his retirement has me thinking again. There's so much I want to do before I retire, so many projects unfinished (or even unstarted).

Another friend of mine is dying. He knows it isn't long. He has lived a long and good life, filled with adventure and love and accomplishment. Yet he still looks forward, to a new Heaven and a new earth, where "there will be no more death or mourning or crying or pain" (Revelation 21:4).

His body is weak, but his mind is alert.

His "earthly tent" is gradually crumbling, but he isn't worried. He is ready for his "eternal house in heaven."

While his flesh is weakening, yet is he strong, with a strength not his own.

Notes

[1]*Tom Landry, An Autobiography*, with Gregg Lewis (Grand Rapids: Zondervan Publishing House; and New York: Harper Collins Publishers, 1990), pp. 148, 149.

[2]John Haggai, *Lead On* (Waco: Word Books, 1986), pp. 38, 39.

[3]Excerpted in John Sharnik, *Inside the Cold War* (New York: Arbor House, 1987), pp. 291, 292.

[4]*Leadership*. Published by Christianity Today. Winter, 1987, p. 123.

[5]Quoted in Leonard Ravenhill, *Why Revival Tarries* (Minneapolis: Bethany House, 1959), p. 28.

[6]Quoted by John Haggai, *Lead On* (Waco: Word Books, 1986), p. 26.

[7]From Alan Loy McGinnis, *Bringing Out the Best in People* (Minneapolis: Augsburg Publishing House, 1985), pp. 38, 39.

12

WITH A LITTLE HELP FROM MY FRIENDS

Luke 15

People need people. Throughout this book we've noticed how often the strength we need comes from other people. Whenever I speak with anyone about accepting Christ as Lord, I immediately move to a discussion of the church. They can't be Christians alone, I explain. They need to be a part of a support group, which is what the church is. Within the church they will find friendship and acceptance and love—and strength.

I never apologize when talking about the social dimension of the Christian life. People are created for society. We cannot live life to the fullest without bonding with other people.

All three parables Jesus tells in Luke 15 have something in common that points out our need for people. In each case, something valuable has been lost. In every case, the lost was found without any help from outsiders. It was after the reunion that the need for others was most keenly felt.

In the first parable, when the shepherd searches out and finally finds the missing sheep, he "calls his friends and neighbors together and says, *'Rejoice with me*; I have found my lost sheep'" (Luke 15:6, italics mine).

In the second, a woman who has ten silver coins loses one. She lights a lamp, she sweeps the house, she searches carefully until she finds that lost coin. "And when she finds it, she calls her friends and neighbors together and says *'Rejoice with me*; I have found my lost coin'" (Luke 15:9, italics mine).

We begin to catch on. You may be able to do many things by yourself, but you can't rejoice by yourself.

Lest we miss the point, Jesus tells one more story, this one of a "lost" son. The father (who represents God in the story, as earlier the shepherd and the woman represented Him) has two sons, an obedient elder son who stays home to work with his father and a rebellious younger one who demands his inheritance now. This his father reluctantly gives. The young man leaves home and squanders his inheritance, undoubtedly breaking his father's heart.

After his entire inheritance passes through his hands, the young man comes "to himself." A good Jew has no business slopping pigs. He is broke, friendless, and homesick. He makes up his mind to return home and face the consequences. Nothing there can be as bad as cohabiting with hogs. Swallowing his pride, he returns. His first words to his father are these:

"Father, I have sinned against heaven and against you. I am no longer worthy to be called your son" (Luke 15:21).

It's his parent's response that is important to our study. Instead of scolding or demanding some kind of reparation, he calls for a party.

> But the father said to the servants, "Quick! Bring the best robe and put it on him. Put a ring on his finger and sandals on his feet. Bring the fatted calf and kill it. Let's have a feast and celebrate. For this son of mine was dead and is alive again; he was lost and is found." *So they began to celebrate* (Luke 15:22-24, italics mine).

Celebrating demands other people.

Worship of God is, among other things, the celebration of new life in Christ. It is giving glory to the One to whom glory is due, praise to whom praise is due. Yes, you can worship somewhat by yourself, in your own home, but full-blown celebration requires being in the presence of others who share your enthusiasm.

Good news belongs to community. As Ralph Sockman wisely puts it,

> A . . . way whereby we lock ourselves out of tomorrow's larger life is by stressing what belongs to us rather than what we belong to. A man's life consisteth not in "the abundance of things which he possesseth" (Luke 12:15). Rather, it consists far more in the abundance and quality of the things to which he belongs.[1]

Life Consists in What We Belong To — or Whom

Christians belong to Christ, but ours is not an exclusive relationship. When we belong to Him, we discover to our delight that to be in Christ is to be in the body of Christ. To be a disciple of Jesus is to be a companion of Jesus' disciples; to be His friend is to be a friend of His friends.

Jesus models the social nature of the Christian faith in His ministry. Somebody pointed out to me the fact that His ministry began in a party and ended at a picnic. He was a very social being, a prophet as unlike the solitary John the Baptist as He could be. His first miracle was performed at the wedding feast in Cana of Galilee. And His final one is recorded in John's Gospel. In a remarkable post-resurrection appearance, after directing His disciples to an extraordinary catch of fish, He hosted a campfire breakfast. From start to finish of His ministry, Jesus lived the social life He expects His disciples to enjoy. Theirs is to be a life of joy, and you can't be joyful alone.

In Anne Tyler's *Breathing Lessons*, Serena invited all her old friends to her husband's funeral, which she had carefully orchestrated as a memorial to earlier, happier times. The songs at the funeral were the songs sung at hers and

Max's wedding; even the singers were the same, though much older and shakier of voice. The funeral guests had also been their wedding guests. She even showed the movie picture of the wedding at the funeral reception. (She referred to it as "my wedding," rather than "ours.") Maggie, her friend, comments on Serena's efforts to treat everything as if time had stopped still, back then, when she had friends.

"Like a very young girl, she had summoned all her high-school friends around her—no one from a later time, no one from the dozen small towns Max had lugged her to during their marriage, for they hadn't stayed in any of those places long enough."

For Maggie, "that [summoning of her high-school friends] was the saddest thing about this whole event."[2] It seemed Serena hadn't made a new friend since, and now in the most severe crisis of her life, she had to turn to her earlier and long-neglected companions and her old memories because they were all she had. Life stopped for her when she stopped making new friends. Without current friendships, she was weak.

Friendship (more often called *fellowship* in the church) is how the Christian faith expresses itself. Even the Lord's Supper symbolizes friendship, doesn't it? The very word *communion* points to something held in common, something shared. You cannot come to the Table without being conscious of the others there with you.

The same social dimension is expressed in baptism, which symbolizes a person's union with Christ—and with the body of Christ. In our congregation, a tradition has spontaneously attached itself to our public baptisms. When the candidate is lifted out of the water, the whole church applauds. This behavior is a little hard on some of us old-timers who were brought up to be reverently silent at such a moment, but we're adjusting because we, too, sense the need to find an acceptable alternative to shouting "Hurrah!" We're excited. Someone who was "lost" has been found. It's time to throw a party. And we can't properly celebrate without each other! We are cheering because somebody has not only come to Christ but has come to us as well. Ours is a social faith. Without each other we are weak.

How Do I Make Friends?

Surprisingly, even within the church, many persons feel alienated. What I have been saying in this chapter is no comfort to them; instead, it exacerbates their loneliness. They haven't found it possible, or at least easy, to make friends in the body.

It isn't hard to find advice on how to make friends. Here is some I found in David Schwartz's popular book, *The Magic of Thinking Big*:[3]

1. Introduce yourself to others at every possible opportunity— at parties, meetings, on airplanes, at work, everywhere.

2. Be sure the other person gets your name straight.

3. Be sure you can pronounce the other person's name the way he pronounces it.

4. Write down the other person's name, and be mighty sure you have spelled it correctly; people have a fetish about the correct spelling of their own names! If possible, get his address and phone number, also.

5. Drop a personal note or make a phone call to the new friends you feel you want to know better. This is an important point. Most successful people follow through on new friends with a letter or a phone call.

6. And last but not least, say pleasant things to strangers. It warms you up and gets you ready for the task ahead.

This is not very profound stuff. You see lists like this one in magazines and books all the time. I selected Schwartz's because it is so typical. An extremely important truth informs his suggestions, however. Of the six points, four of them cause you to focus on other persons, not to possess or manipulate or dominate, but to please, to bring a little joy into their lives.

We fail in making new friends because we want them for *us*, to please *us*, for *ourselves*. But the real art of friendship is in turning our attention outward, doing what we can for *them*. My advice to anyone needing more friends is simple: think about them more than about you. (Jesus would call this loving your neighbor as yourself.)

Will My New Friends Make a Difference in My Life?

There's no doubt about it: your friends do make a difference in your life. Friends unite and friends divide. James says our choice of friends is a spiritual concern: "You adulterous people, don't you know that friendship with the world is hatred toward God? Anyone who chooses to be a friend of the world becomes an enemy of God" (James 4:4).

Powerful language, isn't it? James is drawing on an inherent quality of friendship: a friend sticks. If your friends are given to worldly ways, you stick by them. But to stick with them often requires you to pull away from people devoted to spiritual things.

You already know this. Though you don't use the term *worldly* or *spiritual* to describe your friends, you have still experienced the uniting and dividing aspect of friendship. Because you have chosen certain friends, you cannot have other friends as your intimates. They cannot get along with each other; one is jealous of or despises the other. You can't put them together in the same room for any length of time. Their values fight, even if they don't. So you have to make a choice. They force you to.

Friends Hold Each Other Up

As far as Jesus is concerned, true friends hold nothing back: "Greater love has no one than this, that he lay down his life for his friends" (John 15:13). Friends not only hold each other up, but sacrifice themselves if necessary.

When Mark Hollenbach, one of our associate pastors, led us in the Communion meditation one Sunday, he gave us the perfect example of the power of friendship. He was talking about the Boston Marathon, that absurdly gruelling 26-mile, 365-yard race. I myself have never been tempted to indulge, but I am much impressed by the people who do. Their course is fiendishly designed to be about as hard as possible. After the contestants have run twenty-two miles, they confront a two-mile upgrade before the course levels off for the last couple of miles. This little upgrade is called "Heartbreak Hill."

Prior to the 1987 race, Jim Kelly, an ESPN television announcer, interviewed former runner Bob Varsha. "After running twenty-two miles," he asked, "how do the runners make it up Heartbreak Hill?"

Bob's answer, as Mark related it to us, says it all. "They make it by feeding off the communion they share as they all strain up Heartbreak Hill together."

Communion. That's the word. It is the *communion of spirits* that holds people up when they struggle toward a common goal, too exhausted to make it on their own. That *communion* has blessed me all my life in the church. As a Christian, I have never felt I was having to strain up Heartbreak Hill alone because I've always sensed that in my *community* of believers were other people who cared that I make it to the finish line, as I care that they do.

When Dr. Scott Peck spoke to a nurses' convention in Phoenix, I attended as a guest. A fine psychiatrist and writer, Dr. Peck explored with us the theme on which he was currently researching and writing: community. His prime example was Alcoholics Anonymous. He gave us three reasons for the program's success.

1. It is the only program there is for conversion, one that draws on a "higher power." "Conversion is essential," he said, "for people to overcome their addictions."

2. It is a psychological program. It shows people how and why to go through the desert of their addictive experience. It is "psycho-therapeutic": it meets their psychological needs.

3. It works because of community. People don't have to go through the desert alone. Everybody in the community is battling the same problem. (And so, in communion, they help each other up Heartbreak Hill.)

As Peck talked, I couldn't help reflecting on the Christian life. For Christians, also, the communion we have with the Lord and each other, coupled with the ongoing celebration of life together, gets us up any Heartbreak Hill. From this communion (and celebration), even the weakest gains strength to carry on.

Gordon Cosby, the founding pastor of the Church of the Savior in Washington, D. C., tells of an experience one weekend when he was a guest minister in a New England church. The service was so dull and uninspiring he and his wife left church depressed.

They drove toward home for a while before turning in for the night. When they were ready to retire, the only room they could find was in a wayside inn, above the tavern. They didn't get much sleep that night, he said, because they lay in their bed listening to the happy sounds of laughter and camaraderie coming up from the room below. It was a little hard for Cosby to take.

> I realized that there was more warmth and fellowship in that tavern than there was in the church. If Jesus of Nazareth had his choice he would probably have come to the tavern rather than to the church we visited.[4]

A kind of startling thought, isn't it? Cosby is probably correct. Jesus did not come to proclaim a dull, uninspired, uninspiring way of life. He went to parties, He hosted picnics, He drew people to Him by the warmth of His personality. He modeled friendship and communion of spirit. I can't believe He ever intended for His church to be a drab place for dull people.

I do not mean to imply—and neither did Pastor Cosby —that all taverns are warm and friendly or that all churches are cold. That isn't true. But I do want to tell one more "cold church" story because the church must always be alert to the onset of morbidity.

Leonard Griffith says this really happened to a friend of his, who visited a church in a strange town for Sunday morning service. The church offered many empty pews; but he was a friendly fellow, so he chose a pew near a lady sitting by herself. He had, of course, already taken off his hat; but when he put it on the seat beside him, she leaned over and whispered, "That's my husband's seat." He quickly apologized and moved his hat.

Throughout the service the place remained vacant. He commented afterward, "Your husband didn't come."

"My husband is dead," she said.

So, I suspect, is her church. Very little friendship there.

What Do Friends Do?

By now it should be pretty clear that friends give us strength to carry on, a reason for and a joy in striving. A moment at the close of the Revolutionary War illustrates the virtue of these strength-giving relationships.

On June 11, 1783, Joseph Martin and the men of his company were in their barracks when the captain, bearing an armload of discharge papers, announced the end of the war. They could go home. He made them empty all their cartridge boxes on the floor. Then he told those who needed them to take them back again. That was their pay. Martin, who felt as much sadness as joy at the breaking up of his company, wrote,

> We had lived together as a family of brothers for several years, setting aside some little family squabbles, like most other families, had shared with each other the hardships,

dangers, and sufferings incident to a soldier's life; had sympathized with each other in trouble and sickness; had assisted in bearing each other's burdens or strove to make them lighter by council and advice; had endeavored to conceal each other's faults or make them them appear in as good light as they would bear.[5]

They were, in short, friends.

Crisis continues to bind us together. During the recent Mideast crisis, even non-religious persons told radio reporters of their visits to church. Did they go for prayer alone, or to be with others who shared their concern? Why do people turn to religion when they or someone they love is in trouble? The answer is found in the word. *Religion* derives from the same root as *ligature*. Being "religious" means being "bound" to God; it also means being bound to one another. Religion has to do with community. It means being "one in the Spirit." Going to church in a crisis brings peace, hope, and strength in a communion of spirit. The church is a community. In its embrace, otherwise lonely people find acceptance and friendship.

There is strength in that friendship.

Notes

[1]Ralph Sockman, *Live for Tomorrow* (New York: The Macmillan Company, 1939), p. 105. Italics mine.

[2]Anne Tyler, *Breathing Lessons* (New York: Alfred A. Knopf, 1988), pp. 73, 74.

[3]David Schwartz, *The Magic of Thinking Big* (Cornerstone Library, 1959), pp. 126, 127.

[4]Quoted in Ernest Campbell, *Locked in a Room With Open Doors* (Waco: Word Books, 1974), p. 159.

[5]Page Smith, *A People's History of the American Revolution: A New Age Now Begins*, Volume II (New York, et al: McGraw-Hill, 1976), pp. 1786, 1787.

13

Let God's Power
Be Your Strength

2 Corinthians 13:1-10

We began our study of the "strength not our own" in the twelfth chapter of 2 Corinthians. We end it just across the page, in the thirteenth. The apostle Paul is still defending himself against critics who deny his apostleship and disdain his authority. We can't help noticing in this section of his defense that the words of our study come up repeatedly:

> This will be my third visit to you. "Every matter must be established by the testimony of two or three witnesses." I already gave you a warning when I was with you the second time. I now repeat it while absent: On my return I will not spare those who sinned earlier or any of the others, since you are demanding proof that Christ is speaking through me. He is not *weak* in dealing with you, but is powerful among you. For to be sure, he was crucified in *weakness*, yet he lives by God's *power*. Likewise, we are *weak* in him, yet by God's power we will live with him to serve you.
> Examine yourselves to see whether you are in the faith; test yourselves. Do you not realize that Christ Jesus is in you--unless, of course, you fail the test? And I trust that you will discover that we have not failed the test. Now we pray to God that you will not do anything wrong. Not that people will see that we have stood the test but that you will do what is right even though we may seen to have failed. For we

149

cannot do anything against the truth, but only for the truth. We are glad whenever we are *weak* but you are *strong*; and our prayer is for your perfection. This is why I write these things when I am absent, that when I come I may not have to be harsh in my use of authority—the authority the Lord gave me for building you up, not for tearing you down" (2 Corinthians 13:1-10, italics mine).

"Christ . . . is not weak . . . but is powerful among you." "We are weak in him, yet by God's power we will live." We are *weak*, but He is *strong*. There is for us, indeed, a strength not our own. Sometimes it is called "God's power," as in verse 4, or "Christ in you," as in 5. More often it is spoken of throughout the New Testament as the Holy Spirit's dwelling and working within you.

You have nearly finished reading this book. It's possible that you're still unpersuaded. You've heard me out, nodded politely when you've agreed with some little thing I've said, but still aren't convinced that the strength I've been talking about can make any difference in your life. You may, in fact, be like some of the folks in my congregation who have heroically withstood twelve years of my preaching without changing their minds one bit.

Experience has taught me that some people are quite content in their weakness, just as there are others who really do enjoy their ill health. If you are one of them, let me help you. I can give you. . . .

Four Keys for Maintaining Personal Weakness

They are found in 2 Corinthians 13:1-3.

First, **never put your faith to the test**.

That way you'll never know your true spiritual condition. Paul says, "Examine yourself and see whether you are in the faith; test yourselves. Do you not realize that Christ Jesus is in you—unless, of course, you fail the test?"

He may not be in you. You may just think you really believe Him. How will you know, unless you take Him at

His word and really make up your mind to obey His commands? You may feel pretty good about the church you belong to and the weekly religious rites you put yourself through and be quite oblivious to the fact that some of your cherished beliefs are wrong. Faith is like a muscle: you either strengthen it through exercise or it atrophies, becoming weak and finally useless. Test it.

Test *what you believe*. Is it the truth? How do you know? Is it in harmony with God's revealed Word? How familiar are you with God's revealed Word? Some people have been shocked to discover that some of their favorite Scriptures ("Cleanliness is next to godliness"; "Honesty is the best policy"; "What goes around comes around"; "Neither a borrower nor a lender be") are not in the Bible. Where did you get what you believe?

Then test *your attitude*. Do you feel right about the right things? Is your attitude toward other people Christlike? Can you really love your neighbor—and your enemy—as Jesus requires?

Put yourself to an *aptitude test*. Are you exercising the aptitudes God gave you (sometimes called "spiritual gifts"), using them for His glory? Are you becoming more skillful in applying those gifts?

The tests are designed to help you discover whether you are doing Christlike things with Christlike power or are operating on a merely human level, hampered by all the limitations to which the flesh is subject.

I go back so often in my imagination to that famous scene on the Sea of Galilee when the disciples spotted Jesus walking on the water and one of the disciples, just one, tested his faith. "Lord," Peter said, "Lord, if it's you, tell me to come to you on the water" (Matthew 14:28). And he walked on the water. Say what you want to about Peter's impulsiveness, his failure to look before he leapt, and all that; the fact remains, he wasn't afraid to test his faith. The other disciples? They sat in the boat, protecting their weakness.

A Scripture often read at Communion warns Christians to test their faith in another way.

> Therefore, whoever eats the bread or drinks the cup of the Lord in an unworthy manner will be guilty of sinning against the body and blood of the Lord. A man ought to examine himself before he eats of the bread and drinks of the cup. For anyone who eats and drinks without recognizing the body of the Lord eats and drinks judgment on himself. That is why many among you are weak and sick, and a number of you have fallen asleep (1 Corinthians 11:27-30).

What could failing to examine oneself before partaking of Communion possibly have to do with weakness, sickness, and death? It seems such a little thing, doesn't it, this taking part in the Lord's Supper? Or is it? Could Paul be warning against treating one's relationship with the Lord in a routine, ritualistic way, thus robbing oneself of the strength He wants to impart? Instead of an opportunity to commune with the Lord, drawing power from respectful closeness to Him, one just observes ceremony that Christians do on Sunday. If it's merely ritual, there's no power in it.

So if you want to remain weak in what and how you believe and in what and how you feel and act toward others and in what you can do and how you can do it, never put yourself to the test.

Second, **devote yourself to wrong and not to right**. Paul says it so simply: "Now we pray to God that you will not do anything wrong" (2 Corinthians 13:7). He almost sounds as if he's talking to children, although it's really not such a bad way to talk to adults, is it?

I'm thinking of a couple of them right now, men old enough to know better, who have been hurt and are determined to get even. Oh, they don't call it that. They aren't after vengeance, they would assure you; all they want is justice. They merely want what's coming to them, they'll tell you. Unfortunately, what's coming to them is what they'll get. Their poisonous attitudes are making them weaker and weaker.

Whether it's "getting even" or making an unfair profit at somebody else's expense or cheating on your spouse or stealing from the boss or whatever else it is, when you know what's right and you compromise your standards, you'll grow increasingly ineffective and powerless in life. You may justify and rationalize and excuse yourself until you think you have convinced yourself, but you can never quite get away with it—unless you have gone so far that you've made yourself morally sick. There is no way to devote yourself to wrong and make yourself strong.

The third key to maintaining personal weakness is this one: **Lie your way through life.** Here's what Paul says: "For we cannot do anything against the truth, but only for the truth" (2 Corinthians 13:8).

Most of us think of ourselves as being basically honest. Like Huckleberry Finn, we tell the truth—mostly. We're not guilty of telling any really horrendous lies, the kind of lies that land politicians in the headlines. No, we aren't guilty of that. We're more prone to the little white lies, the April 15 kind of lies. We almost tell the truth on our tax returns. (Is there any better test of our integrity than this?)

The problem with little white lies is in their cumulative effect. They add up. In time, they define character. Strong persons don't have to bend the truth.

If it's weakness you want, lie your way through life.

The fourth key to maintaining personal weakness is this one: **Go to work against somebody**. Paul writes: "We are glad whenever we are weak but you are strong; and our prayer is for your perfection" (2 Corinthians 13:9). Isn't that a wonderful sentence? If you think of me as weak, Paul tells them, that's okay. Think of me as weak because I'm really not thinking of me right now. What I really care about is that you are strong.

As Christians, we are not called into competition with one another. And we are certainly forbidden to be enemies of one another in Christ. Let's read the next sentence because it's so clear here:

> This is why I write these things when I am absent, that when I come I may not have to be harsh in my use of authority— the authority the Lord gave me for building you up, not for tearing you down (2 Corinthians 13:10).

The only authority the Lord has ever given you and me is for the purpose of building others up. We have no right to tear another person down. Ever. To do so is to go against the expressed will of God—and in this contest between His strength and ours, who do you think will win? So when we set about to destroy somebody by tongue or deed, we've taken our stand against God. We have guaranteed our own weakness.

So far I've been treating this chapter negatively, to help any reader who prefers weakness to strength. I hope you're not one of them. Believing you aren't (or you wouldn't have stayed with me for thirteen chapters), let me take us back through this same passage again, this time to emphasize the positive.

Four Keys for Attaining Personal Strength

The first key for gaining personal strength is this: **Put your faith to the test.** As we observed earlier, our faith must be tested; otherwise we don't know how strong we are or what kind of faith we have. It's only when the going gets rough, it is only when the world seems to fall in on us, that we know whether we have faith or not. There isn't any virtue in a faith that is never put to the test. You don't know whether you can love your enemy until he attacks and you have a chance to respond. You don't know whether you can trust the Lord until hard times beset you. So, Paul says, "Put your faith to the test."

Some years ago I read a book on architectural engineering. I didn't know the first thing about the subject (still don't know much), which is the reason I bought the book. I can't tell you that I learned a great deal—except for one lesson that was repeated again and again in the book. Have you ever wondered how engineers know just how long to make the span of the bridge? I can tell you. The book taught me. Engineers know just how long the span can be by going just beyond the limit. When the bridge falls down, they know they went too far. They put their theory to the test; when it failed, they backed up this side of the limit.

In visiting those magnificent Gothic cathedrals in Europe, I've stood and looked up in amazement at the ascending heights of the structures and wondered, "How did the medieval architects and engineers determine how high to lift these towers into the sky? How did they know how far up they could go without having the whole edifice come crashing down?" The book told me. It said they kept building them higher and higher until, inevitably, one of them collapsed. Then they said, "Well, we can't go that high any more." That's how they learned it. They put their faith to the test.

I'm not suggesting we court disaster, you understand. The point is that architectural engineers, had they not tested their theories (as the Scriptures suggest we Christians test our faith), they could never have built the spanning bridges and towering cathedrals. And none of the scientific and technological achievements we take for granted in the twentieth century could have occurred. Yes, sometimes they went too far, but what if they hadn't gone at all?

Of course, you and I will make some mistakes as we put our faith to the test. But how else will we know how far we can go?

In this respect we're like children learning to walk. It's not always fun, is it, for the parents? When the children are learning to walk, they fall and they fall and they fall. The falling is a very important part of learning to walk, isn't it? And you don't stop them from trying, do you? You know that without the risk there will be no walking. In time, they teach themselves how far to go and what to touch. They learn, for example, not to put their fingers in the electric socket, often by putting their fingers in the electric socket! Growth is made up of risk and hurt and trial and error.

We readily acknowledge this is true of how children grow. What happens to us when we become adults

If you want to grow stronger, put your faith to the test.

God even invites us to put him to the test, according to the prophet Malachi. He was talking about tithing, which some believers in God still find to be a strenuous, almost impossibly demanding test of their faith. God calls it a test of himself, as well as of believers. "Test me in this [in bringing the whole tithe into the storehouse] . . . and see if I will not throw open the floodgates of heaven and pour out so much blessing that you will not have room enough for it" (Malachi 3:10).

There you have it. If you want to grow stronger, put yourself (and the Lord) to the test.

We who are in the middle years of life start conserving our strength, protecting our assets, withdrawing from activities requiring much expenditure of energy. "I'm getting older," we say to ourselves, partly as excuse and partly because we really think we are. We begin to sound as if all the gusto of life is behind us. What damage we do ourselves. (I write as one smack in the middle of the middle.) Now is the time we ought to be stretching more than ever. We know—nobody has to tell us—that these bodies of ours don't have all the resilience they once had, but what about the person who inhabits the body? Is it all over for him or her?

I love Paul's words in 2 Corinthians 4. Having spoken of the glorious privilege of preaching Christ, he describes the fragile preacher: "We have this treasure in jars of clay to show that this all-surpassing power is from God and not from us" (2 Corinthians 4:7).

What's so good about being middle-aged is that people like us have finally realized that whatever power we have, power that's good for something and worth talking about, isn't ours anyway. We know what Paul's talking about. Yet—and this is going to sound familiar by now—it is when we admit our weakness that God's power can work through us.

That is why we aren't afraid to put our faith to the test, because our faith isn't in ourselves but in the one who is All-powerful. What He wants us to do, He gives us the energy to do!

The second key to attaining personal strength: **devote yourself to right and not to wrong.** These first two keys are an unbeatable combination: Test your faith in Him by putting your energies into the things that you know are right.

Wasn't it President Woodrow Wilson, facing certain defeat in his attempt to get the United States to enter the League of Nations, who said that he would rather fail in a cause he knew someday would succeed than succeed in a cause he knew someday would fail? Nothing energizes a person more than wholehearted devotion to a just and lasting cause.

When is that "someday" that Wilson mentions? To every man and woman that someday will come, when life's days on earth are ended and the accounting is made of the stewardship of one's days. Have you ever wondered what people are going to say of you when you're gone? Will due note be taken of the fact that you devoted your life to what will last, what will ultimately succeed? What will be said at your funeral? Will you then, in your final weakness, appear to have lived well or poorly? Will you be praised for having made a lot of money or never had a critic or never caused waves? Or for having given yourself away, recklessly even, for something really worth living and dying for?

Devote yourself to the right and not the wrong.

The third key to personal strength: **never try to lie your way through life**. The truth will come out.

Remember the crowd on Palm Sunday, singing and chanting and praising the One coming in the name of the Lord, and the Pharisees grumbling and ordering Jesus to shut them up. He didn't. He couldn't, He said. You can't shut up the truth. As a result, that Palm Sunday song has never been put out. It cannot be. What did we learn when the Berlin wall came tumbling down? We looked for the first time in decades into Eastern Europe and discovered churches. Through all those years of persecution, faithful, dedicated, sacrificing Christians, in spite of every threat and danger, had adhered to their faith. You can't shut up the truth.

We know the same thing is true in Communist China. We've only recently been learning of the strength of the underground church there, in which people are praising the Lord and studying His Word even though it has been forbidden for generations. The truth will not be put out.

This is in keeping with Jesus' promise: "If you hold to my teaching, you are really my disciples. Then you will know the truth, and the truth will set you free" (John 8:31, 32).

Free from what? Free from fear, for one thing. Free from the fear of being found out. (If you want to be a good liar, you must have a good memory!) Free from defensiveness. Free from envy, jealousy, hatred, bitterness, anger, and all the rest of the consequences of trying to manipulate and compete and cheat your way through life.

It's hard for me to write these lines because my heart hurts for a person I love very much, whose beautiful personality is disintegrating because of a choice to lie rather than to be truthful. This is not an uncommon characteristic of persons afflicted with addictive personalities. The cure requires first of all that the person become truthful. No easy task. For any of us.

The fourth key is one you've heard throughout this book: **work for another, not for yourself.** Strength comes quickly to those who give themselves away.

Isn't Paul's language instructive? "We are glad whenever we are weak but you are strong; and our prayer is for your perfection"(2 Corinthians 13:9). We are strong, he implies, when we work for your perfection, even though we may appear to be weak.

There's a woman in the church I serve of whom I have written before. She can get me to do any job she wants. I wouldn't know how to turn her down, but not because she is domineering. No, she's the opposite, as a matter of fact. What commands my obedience is the woman's spirit of servanthood. I've known her for twelve years now, and during that time she has never asked anything for herself. Her concern is always for others. If you were to ask me to list the persons in my church according to their personal strength, I would have to put her at the top of the list. She's powerful — for others.

If I could ask the readers of this book to name the one celebrity in the world today whom you would consider to be the most dynamic, powerful personality, I have no doubt that the votes would come in overwhelmingly for no political or military leader, but instead for a little lady not five feet tall who works among the dying in the slums of India. Mother Teresa has captured the imagination of the whole world. We admire her, we praise her — but we wouldn't imitate her for anything. We're not as strong as she! Beyond a doubt, she has found the secret of strength.

You can too. Let me give you a couple more Scriptures and then I must bring this book to a close. Here's a well-known one, Psalm 37:3, 4.

Trust in the Lord and do good;
  dwell in the land and enjoy safe pasture.

Delight yourself in the Lord
    and he will give you the desires of your heart.

When you want what He wants, when you think what He thinks, when you love as He loves, when you delight in what He delights in, He'll give you what you want out of life. His strength will energize you.

The other Scripture takes us back where we began, just across the page to the twelfth chapter. You'll remember we began this study talking about thorns in the flesh. Let's think about them one last time:

> To keep me from becoming conceited because of these surpassingly great revelations, there was given me a thorn in my flesh, a messenger of Satan, to torment me. Three times I pleaded with the Lord to take it away from me. But he said to me, *"My grace is sufficient for you, for my power is made perfect in weakness."* Therefore, I will boast all the more gladly about my weaknesses, so that Christ's power may rest on me. That is why, for Christ's sake, I delight in weaknesses, in insults, in hardships, in persecutions, in difficulties. *For when I am weak, then I am strong* (2 Corinthians 12: 7-10, italics mine).

So we stop where we started, conscious of our personal weaknesses but even more conscious of His power.
His grace is sufficient.
When we are weak, then we are strong.